FINDING FAYE

Intuitive Investigator Series: Book Two

Deanne Acuña
with
Sue Phillips

Sweetbriar Creek Publishing Company

HENDERSON, NEVADA

Sweetbriar Creek Publishing Company
PO Box 92683
Henderson, NV 89009

www.SuePhillipsAuthor.com

Publisher's Note: This is a work of nonfiction. Names, characters and places have been changed to protect the innocent and deny notoriety to the guilty. Locales and public names are sometimes used for atmospheric purposes. Any resemblance to actual businesses, companies, institutions, or locales may be completely coincidental.

Book Cover Design © 2014 HotDamnDesigns.com
Book Layout © 2014 BookDesignTemplates.com

Finding Faye: Intuitive Investigator Bk 2/ Deanne Acuña with Sue Phillips
1st edition
ISBN 978-1-941428-04-7

IN MEMORY OF

George A. "Pete" Getz
The love of my life

CONTENTS

FOREWORD

The California Legislature defined human trafficking as "all acts involved in the recruitment, abduction, transport, harboring, transfer, sale or receipt of persons, within national or across international borders, through force, coercion, fraud or deception, to place persons in situations of slavery or slavery-like conditions, forced labor or services, such as forced prostitution or sexual services, domestic servitude, bonded sweatshop labor, or other debt bondage."—State of California Senator, Kamala D. Harris

Human trafficking is one of the fastest growing crimes in the world. The average age of entry for children in twelve years. Approximately eighty percent of the victims are women and girls. Many are fearful to seek help because of their immigration status or prostitution arrests. Human trafficking is both a federal and a state crime, punishable by life in prison.

Orange County, California has a task force and has assisted victims of human trafficking since 2004.

https://www.egovlink.com/ochumantrafficking/

For further information: The National Human Trafficking Resource (NHTR) hotline number is 1-888-373-7888.

https://traffickingresourcecenter.org/.

According to the NHTR statistics, California has the highest reported cases of human trafficking in the United

States.

NHTR website is funded by the Anti-Trafficking in Persons Division (ATIP), Office of Refugee Resettlement, U.S. Department of Health and Human Services. ATIP "identifies and serves victims of human trafficking, assisting foreign trafficking victims in the United States to become eligible for public benefits and services to the same extent as refugees."

The investigative case you are about to read took place in 1990, long before the above-named organizations had been formed to help victims and families searching for them. The names have been changed to protect everyone involved in the case.

CHAPTER 1

August 1, 1990
Wednesday, 9:00 a.m.
Long Beach, California

Her teenage daughter had been missing for six weeks.

My heart sank. I held the phone to my ear, listening to Ida Franklin. I felt her weary desperation deep inside my chest.

"My husband and I have flown to Cancun twice to search for her," she said. "The local authorities have told us that they have done all they can do. We hired a couple of private investigators down there, but neither of us is fluent in Spanish so we're not even sure if they did anything other than take our money. After we came home, I spoke to Brian Masson here in New Hampshire. He sympathized with our circumstances but didn't have the ability to take an international case. He remembers meeting you through the national organization of legal investigators."

"Yes, that would be NALI. Brian and I served on a committee together a few years ago. He's highly qualified and I would recommend him to anyone. He also knows I'm bilingual and certified as an international investigator, which takes him out of his realm of expertise."

"To be perfectly honest, my husband and I never considered hiring a woman. For safety reasons, that is." She cleared her throat. "I don't mean to offend."

"No offense taken." In front of me, on my desk, was a framed photo of my son and daughter from last Christmas. Michael is in college. Kitty, a high school senior. I ran my finger along the frame's edge. "I'm a mother, too. If I were in your situation, I would want the best of the best."

"Mr. Masson said *you* are the best he's ever met. He claimed you find people when no one else can. Is that true?"

"More often than not." I am proud of my success rate, though I don't like to make a big deal over it. Nor do I talk openly about my psychic abilities. I prefer to keep those to myself unless someone specifically asks about them. Instead, I let my record speak for itself. "Before I commit to taking a case, I do my own preliminary investigation to weigh the risks. Safety is a reasonable concern for anyone involved, man or woman. Your daughter's situation will probably require a team of several investigators."

"Whatever is involved to get our daughter back, we'll pay for it."

"First, I need information about your daughter and the friends who were with her in Cancun. Please be honest with me." I took out a legal pad and pen. "Has she ever taken off on her own before?"

"No. Never. Faye isn't that type of person. We've never had any trouble with her. She's a wonderful daughter. She's not reckless or impulsive. She's extremely responsible with a good head on her shoulders. She called every day to check in to let us know she was safe. The last time we heard from her she was having the time of her life. She's an excellent student and was looking forward to starting NYU in the fall."

"When did she disappear?"

"June twentieth. A few hours after our last call, the girls went to a night club around the corner from their hotel. Faye danced quite a bit with a particular young man who paid her a great deal of attention. When her friends wanted to go to another club, Faye let the man talk her into staying behind with him. Since the hotel was so close, she assured them she could get back safely on her own."

"Did they get the man's name?"

"Alex. He spoke English without a distinguishable accent so they assumed he was an American tourist like them."

I jotted down the info. "What about a last name?"

"James or Jones. Celia couldn't remember exactly. She took a picture of him with Faye. But they were several feet away and the place was dark. The photograph has been enlarged for a clearer view of his face. That man is behind her disappearance. I'm sure of it."

Her gut instinct was the same as mine. That feeling in the pit of my stomach is a sure sign. Every time I trusted it, I've been glad I did.

"I want to be clear that no one has asked for a ransom. Correct?"

"Right. Nobody has contacted us."

"Tell me about the friends who went with your daughter." I drew a line under my notes.

"Celia Bracken has been her best friend since first grade. They're like Mutt and Jeff. Faye is five-five in her stocking feet. Celia is five-ten. Faye has brown hair styled into a shoulder-length bob. Celia has very long, very straight blonde hair. Faye is the academic. Celia is the athlete, and much more out-going. She wanted to attend college in California but decided on NYU because of Faye."

Mrs. Franklin's description of her daughter was all that I needed, but I let her talk freely as I wrote down the information. Victims of crime often were in such as state of shock they froze up, unable to articulate any details. Others, like Mrs. Franklin, did the opposite, recalling everything and anything that could possibly help the investigation. Sometimes, a seemingly mundane fact turned out to be important.

"And the others?" I asked.

"Six girlfriends went with Faye to Cancun. Celia, Bonnie Wright, Amanda Canefield, Carla Brontski, Penny Richards and Roxanne Dixon. They are all distraught and feel somewhat responsible for leaving Faye at the club. They're all nice young girls who just graduated from a private school. I've known five of the girls and their families since they started at the school when they were just five years old. Roxanne came to the academy two years ago. I don't know her as well."

"But ...?" My pen continued writing the names.

"Excuse me?"

"I get the sense that you don't like Roxanne."

Mrs. Franklin held her silence for a long moment. "Mr. Masson said you're psychic."

"I have certain abilities, yes. Telepathy being one of them. Actually, your tone changed when you said Roxanne's name."

"Are you reading my mind right now?" she asked.

Her voice sounded slightly alarmed. I knew she needed

assurance. "Not in the way you might think. I don't always know the exact words you are about to say. But the emotion behind the words comes to me. The stronger the emotion, the stronger the mental imagery you project."

"Oh. If I sent you something of Faye's, could you tell us where she is?"

"No. I don't work that way. If you are expecting me to pinpoint her precise location, you will be disappointed. I've trained extensively as an investigator. I run down leads and I go undercover. My intuition guides me, but I also do the legwork. A *lot* of legwork."

"You said telepathy is one of your abilities. What are the others?"

"Precognition. I receive warnings of a death or a major disaster before it happens." Even through the telephone connection, I felt rising fear in Mrs. Franklin. "Before you ask, I don't have anything about your daughter."

My shoulders sagged under a heavy pressure. Disappointment. Not mine, though. I was picking up on the waning energy of Mrs. Franklin on the other side of the continent. The fingers in both my hands ached from the strain of a tight grip on the receiver, even though I held it with one hand while I wrote my notes with the other. The physical telepathy came from Mrs. Franklin.

"Please help us." She sounded on the verge of tears. "Anything you want, we'll give it to you. We love our daughter and we want her back home."

My own throat tightened with hers, and I swallowed hard. I needed to make sure my voice would sound professional.

"Send me photos of her, including the one in the club with the man calling himself Alex James-or-Jones. Also, give me as much information as you have, no matter how insignificant it seems to you. Do you have the phone numbers for the girlfriends?"

"Right here." She read them to me. After the last one, she asked, "Should I send some money as a deposit?"

"Not until I decide to take your case. Please let those friends know I'll be contacting them."

"I guess I have no choice but to be patient. I pray to God you will help us."

"I'm sorry I can't give you a positive answer right now. I'll get back to you in a few days."

After I hung up the telephone, I sat alone with my thoughts. Faye's disappearance was every parent's worst nightmare, including my own.

For over ten years, I've raised my two kids without much help from my ex-husband. The hard times drew me closer to Michael and Kitty, who shares my telepathic ability.

Our psychic connection emerged before she could talk. At six months old, she woke me in the middle of the night with her silent call of distress. I'd found her lying listless and rushed her to the hospital. If I'd slept until morning, the doctors had said, she would have been a victim of SIDS—Sudden Infant Death Syndrome. She and I became so adept at telepathic communication that I'd inadvertently delayed her verbal development. Today, Kitty and I can have entire conversations without realizing we haven't spoken aloud.

Even now, I knew my daughter was thinking of me. I

picked up my office phone on its first ring. "Hi, Sweetheart."

"Hi, Mom. Who's Paul?"

"I know a few guys named Paul. Do you have a last name?"

"No. I just keep getting his first name, and that he has something to do with you. Could he be connected to your friends in Puerto Vallarta?"

I had an extended family, of sorts, in the town that felt like my second home. I visited so often over the years that the Padilla family considered me one of their own.

"Not Paulos?" I asked, referring to the name of the youngest Padilla son.

"Nope. Definitely Paul." She chuckled. "Now I hear a bagpipe."

An image of another investigator popped into my head. He didn't play the bagpipes but the symbol was close enough. "Paul Macintosh?"

"Zing!"

I smiled to myself. When Kitty was little, she would experience a tingling sensation up her spine whenever she had a psychic hit. The only way she knew how to describe it was a "zing" up her back.

In only a couple of seconds, I remembered Paul had worked some investigations in Mexico.

"He's just the person I need to contact about a case that I've been asked to take," I said with a smile. "Thanks, honey. You've been really helpful."

"Any time, Mom. Is it okay if I miss dinner tonight? Terry and I want to catch a movie."

"Sure. I'll pick up something for myself on the way home."

I already knew Michael wouldn't be home. He'd taken a summer job at a popular restaurant in Sunset Beach.

After leaving a message for Paul on his answering machine, I checked my watch. Nine-thirty. I had a meeting with an attorney at one o'clock to hand over my surveillance report on a man claiming to have an incapacitating back injury from an industrial accident that had left him confined to a wheel chair. I'd taken pictures of him walking out of a bar at two in the morning and climbing behind the wheel of his car.

I still had enough time to knock out another report and have a bite to eat at Riley's Deli across the street. I grabbed two sheets of typing paper and a carbon to sandwich between them. Despite the growing popularity of office computers, I still used my Smith-Corona manual typewriter for security reasons. I can't risk having any private information left inside a computer for a technician to discover during repair or maintenance on the machine.

A few minutes later, a quick knock at my door pulled my attention from the report as a tall, good-looking gentleman came into my office.

"I thought I'd pop in to ask you out to lunch."

"Ryan!" I jumped up from my chair, rounded the desk and slid my hands around his waist.

His smile broadened as he pulled me close and kissed me.

We had met during my previous case for a young woman whose oldest brother had murdered her parents and was after her. She needed a new identity but couldn't leave town without her critically injured younger brother. Ryan entered the picture when we needed an auto body shop to change the color of her

Porsche, which she couldn't bring herself to sell as it was a gift from her parents on her last birthday. Ryan ended up also changing the appearance of two vehicles owned by her mother and father.

Lisa and her kid brother eventually relocated to the East Coast while I helped track down the perpetrator, Kevin, in New Mexico. Somewhere along the way, Ryan and I fell in love.

"It's a bit early for lunch," I said to him.

He shrugged. "I had some business downtown this morning. It didn't take as long as I'd expected. I was on my way back to the shop, driving down Broadway, and my car suddenly stalled right in front of this office building."

"Imagine that."

"No good, huh?"

I grinned. "Not buying it."

"In all fairness, I did have business downtown. And I do want to take you to lunch. I can come back later."

I sighed with regret. "I hate to spoil the fun but I'm waiting for a phone call. And I have an appointment with a client at one o'clock."

"Then how about dinner tonight? A new Italian restaurant opened up by my place."

"Sounds wonderful."

At that moment, the phone rang.

"I'd better let you get that," Ryan said, then gave me a quick kiss. "Pick you up at six."

He was out the door by the time I picked up the receiver and recognized Paul's voice. We exchanged pleasantries before

I got down to business, telling him the situation with Mrs. Franklin and her missing daughter.

"Sounds high risk," he finally said. "I wouldn't go to Mexico alone if I were you. I'd offer my services but I'm running two big cases that might take a few months."

"I'm here if you need to talk after you get more information."

"Thanks, Paul. I trust your opinion."

"If you decide to take the case, make sure you have all your ducks in a row."

"Definitely. Ideally, I could use an experienced investigator in Cancun who knows everything about the area. You know— the people, the culture, the police."

"Smart thinking. Get someone who has connections to pull together a team for you.

"Exactly."

"I know a good investigator in Mexico City."

"That's almost five hundred miles away."

"Yes, I know. But I have used him to track down witnesses all over the country and obtain statements from them. I'm sure he'd be a great asset to you."

"I still need to talk to a few more people before I make up my mind about taking the case. But I'd like to speak to him, too."

"His name is Ricardo Perez. Hang on while I get his number."

After receiving Ricardo's information, I thanked Paul and told him I'd keep in touch. I hung up and stared at my notes, ending in the number for Perez. I toyed with the pen like a miniature baton, flipping it around and between my fingers. It's an old habit I fall into when I'm concentrating.

I decided to hold off calling the investigator in Mexico City. No point taking up his time while I was still not sure I could deal with the risks involved. Most people think of Cancun as a vacation resort, not a dangerous place. But I visit friends in Mexico often and knew about the violence and corruption of drug cartels. Beyond the relative safety of the hotels, tourists had to be extra cautious. But search for Faye could draw unwanted attention from her captors if I wasn't careful.

I wanted to help Mrs. Franklin. I wanted to find her daughter. But how far would I be willing to go? Could I put my own life on the line? Would that be fair to my own two children?

CHAPTER 2

August 3, 1990
Friday, 3:00 p.m.

Two days after my phone call with Mrs. Franklin, I received the photograph. But I hadn't been able to obtain new information out of the five girls when I reached them. As expected, they were guilt-ridden, especially Celia. Each cried while giving me the same story Mrs. Franklin had already told me.

The time had come to call Ricardo Perez in Mexico City. Introductions weren't necessary. Paul had already let him know about me, my credentials, and that I might be contacting him.

"Deanne, allow me to be brutally honest. I suspect Faye Franklin was kidnapped to be a sex slave. I worked a similar case a few months ago. They use a good-looking young man to find a naïve young woman, usually but not always at a nightclub. He slips a sedative into her drink. When it takes effect, he carries her unconscious to his car and drives her to a secluded camp where these girls are kept. They are shot up with drugs until they are dependent upon them and will do anything for another fix, even having sex with thirty men in one night."

My stomach clenched. Shocking as the news was, I kept my

reaction to myself. "Did you find the girl in that case?"

"Yes, but I had a hell of a time getting her to cooperate. Heroin was everything to her. She did not care what she had to do to get it. To her, I was the enemy, as was the rest of my team. Going with us meant giving up the high. Together, we managed to extract her and get her back to the United States. Currently, she is under psychiatric care. And she's only twenty years old."

"Do you think we might be successful in locating Faye?"

"I am sorry to say that the odds are stacked against you. More and more, I am hearing these girls are being transported far from the site of their abductions, making tracking them down more difficult. Girls working in Mexico City could have been taken from Tijuana or Guatemala or anywhere else far away."

The image of young girls working the sex trade sickened me. "Anything else I need to know?"

"The search can be expensive. In my last case, I had to pay off several officials. If the parents of this girl cannot afford the cost ... well, chances are slim to none of getting her back."

"You've given me a lot to think about."

"I'll be gone for the next two weeks. If you decide to take the case, I will help you when I return."

I glanced at my calendar and wrote the date on my pad. I couldn't help but think of the Franklins and the agonizing delays in finding their daughter. But the answer was not to rush into the search without preparation. I could only hope they would understand.

"Thank you for your insight."

"Please give my regards to Paul."

"I will. He spoke highly of you. He said if he were me, he wouldn't take the case if you couldn't help. After talking to you, I have to agree. Thanks again, Ricardo. I appreciate your time. I'll call you one way or the other."

After I said goodbye, I leaned back in my desk chair, reluctant to call Mrs. Franklin. The conversation was not one I wanted to have with the mother. No doubt she was having nightmares about her missing daughter. But Ricardo's bleak suspicion would be even more shocking and upsetting. I, myself, was having a hard time with the images of so many young girls being forced into drug addiction to become sex slaves.

Tracking down Faye was one thing. Rescuing her would be extremely dangerous. In my gut, I knew I had to help. I won't deny that the very idea scared me.

My intuition guides me all the time but it's not battle armor. The ability doesn't necessarily keep me out of tough spots, but it warns me in the nick of time. We all have intuition. The trick is to pay close attention. That instinct "talks" to us in many ways, particularly through sensations in our bodies.

Ancient philosophies consider the gut, or belly, the "power center." A strong gut feeling—good or bad—gives us the proverbial power to make a decision. The same can be said about the heart—the center of emotion. For centuries, many cultures believe love emanates from the heart. We also talk of the "heartache" of losing someone.

With my hands resting on my belly, I contemplated the inevitable dialogue with Mrs. Franklin. Admittedly, a few butterflies were inside. I am only human. I wish I could say that I had a clairvoyant vision of the future, assuring me that the circumstances would all work out fine. But I didn't.

However, I do believe that everything happens for a reason, even if we don't realize the synchronicity of events until after they happen. Mrs. Franklin had been sent to me because I have the skills to help her. Call it God. Call it Universal Intelligence. Call it Divine Mind. Call it whatever you want. "It" brought her into my life to help her.

My gut was telling me to accept this case.

But what about my kids? I had a feeling in my heart they would want me to help save Faye. Not to say they wouldn't be worried about my safety. All the more reason why I would be sure to have, as Paul said, "all my ducks in a row."

I sat up, straightened the notepad on the desk, and reached for the phone. Mrs. Franklin picked up after the second ring. She took the news about Ricardo's speculation as well as could be expected. We talked about the problems of investigating in a foreign country. I told her Ricardo said the officials would require payment for helping.

"My husband and I already tried that. Bribes didn't get us anywhere."

"But Mr. Perez knows how to make things happen. He handled a similar missing person case a few months ago."

"Does this mean you're sending us to Mr. Perez instead of taking the case?" she asked.

"No. I would work with him. Following an investigation beyond the U.S. border, particularly in Central America, requires a great deal of coordination that I cannot do alone.

Only a fool would go into a foreign country and expect to know more than local investigators about their own people and culture."

"Yes, of course. I understand. How soon can you start?" Her previous desperation was replaced with a stoic confidence. She believed I was the one who would find Faye.

"Before I give a definite yes, I want to make sure my kids are on board with my decision."

"Oh." She sounded a little surprised but quickly recovered. "How old are they?"

"Michael is twenty. Kitty is eighteen."

"Same age as my daughter."

"Yes." My grip on the phone tightened causing my fingers to ache. I sensed my own maternal anxiety meld with hers. "They need to be aware of the situation before I take the case. I would be leaving the country with no idea how long I will be gone."

"I understand. I just—. She's been missing for so long already. Every day that goes by ..."

"I am sorry to put you through more delays, Mrs. Franklin. But Mr. Perez is tied up with another case for the next two weeks."

"Two weeks?" she echoed. My throat tightened as I felt her constrain her tears of frustration.

"I know this is hard on you and your husband. But I also have to wrap up investigations for my other clients. I will call you as soon as I possibly can."

"We will be waiting by the phone."

I hung up. My hand rested on the receiver. I thought of

Michael and Kitty, wondering what I would do if one of them vanished for one day, let alone six weeks. Making the Franklins wait was difficult for me, but this was real life, not a television crime drama where everything happened in rapid succession.

I wished I could snap my fingers to speed up the process, but I couldn't.

My next step was to talk to my kids.

And Ryan.

CHAPTER 3

Thursday, 5:00 a.m.
Los Angeles International Airport

Michael and Kitty had not hesitated to give their approval of my investigative mission in Mexico. Granted, they were still concerned for my safety, as was Ryan who had offered to take me to the airport. Due to the limited four–hour nonstop flights and the two-hour time difference, my choices were narrowed to an early morning or mid-afternoon departure, neither of which would accommodate the scheduled meeting with Ricardo Perez on Friday. I decided to fly out on Thursday, taking the morning flight that would allow a safe arrival at my hotel long before dark.

The thirty-five-minute drive from my home in Long Beach to LAX in El Segundo could take more than an hour if the morning traffic was particularly heavy, especially along the South Bay curve of the 405 freeway. With the I-105 still under construction, Century Boulevard was the only artery from the freeway to the terminals and was often a slow crawl with weekend travelers. Ryan picked me up two hours before my seven-thirty flight and, surprisingly, we pulled into the short-term parking structure at six-fifteen.

As I climbed out of the low-slung Corvette, I reached for

my purse and my portable cellular phone on the floorboard. Even though the phone's case was as big as a metropolitan Yellow Pages, heavier than a brick and might only get reception in the large cities of Mexico, I never went anywhere without it.

Ryan grabbed my small suitcase from the back of his Corvette. "Are you sure you've brought enough clothes? You had three times this much for our trip to Mexico last November. And that was only two weeks."

"I don't need vacation clothes this time. Just the bare essentials." I didn't know how long I would be gone, but I had to pack as light as possible to simplify whatever traveling I would be doing. The ability to leave at a moment's notice was important while investigating.

"I wish I could go with you," he said, carrying the bag in one hand and slipping his other hand around my waist.

I leaned into him as we walked. "Me, too."

"Say the word, and I'll buy a ticket at the counter."

His offer warmed my heart. "Even if I said yes—which I can't—you don't have anything with you."

An eyebrow lifted. "You didn't see the backpack in the trunk?"

I turned my head and looked up at him. "Don't try to fool me."

"Ah—yes, the mind—reader. How easily I forget." He grinned and pressed a kiss to my forehead. "So, you already know how much I will miss you."

"Not as much as I'll miss you. I'll call you whenever I can."

He only nodded.

We walked together to the check–in counter to get my boarding pass. My bag was small enough to fit in the overhead bin so Ryan carried it with him as we made our way to the Mexicana Airlines gate. We bought coffee and bagels for breakfast from a vendor and sat in the hard plastic seats of the passenger boarding area. We chatted about everything and anything except my pending departure.

Despite the light-hearted conversation, I felt the tension of the last two weeks building to this day when I would finally be on my way to Mexico to start the hunt of Faye Franklin.

When the announcement to board the plane broadcast over the P.A. system, I felt an ache in my chest.

He wrapped his arms around me and held me close, whispering in my ear, "I hope you know how much you mean to me."

"I do." I swallowed hard. "I feel the same way."

He leaned back and cupped my face in his hands. "I love you."

My eyes filled with tears. "I love you, too."

CHAPTER 4

August 17, 1990
Friday, 10:30 a.m.
Mexico City, Mexico

My hotel was in the colonial district of Coyoacán where Ryan and I had stayed during our trip. I have visited the city many times over the years, but everything had been new for Ryan. Sharing the culture and historical sites had given me a chance to show him how much I loved the country, especially the people. The best part of the entire trip was the warm welcome he received from my friends.

Taking a taxi from my hotel to the meeting with Ricardo Perez was as tedious as the ride into town from the airport. The most densely populated city in the world had a traffic problem far worse than Los Angeles. I'm not the most patient person, especially when the cars are moving slower than the pedestrians. If not for the threat of rain, I could have walked to my destination. August is the wettest month of the year. The higher elevation keeps the temperature in the seventies, but the humidity makes the air feel much warmer. Thankfully, the cab's AC worked, and I had allowed for delay.

Seeing a familiar restaurant brought back vivid memories of my time with Ryan, making me miss him terribly. I had only been gone for twenty-four hours. I couldn't start pining for my lover already, especially when I didn't know how long I would be searching for Faye Franklin. Several weeks could pass before I returned home.

The missing young woman was never far from my thoughts, despite the reminiscence of happier times in this city. Ricardo had talked of abducted girls transported far away from their original location. Could Faye have been brought here to Mexico City from Cancun?

I gazed out the window of the slow-moving taxi, watching the people and studying the windows and doors of the buildings. Intuitively, I did not sense her presence or anything else to guide me in the search. However, I did not rule out the possibility of Faye being in the city.

The taxi driver interrupted my thoughts, asking in English if I was enjoying my first visit. He noticed my intense scrutiny of the neighborhood and assumed I was a tourist. I answered in Spanish that I was on a business trip and smiled at his look of surprise reflected in his rear view mirror.

"¿No es Americana? ¡Es Argentino!" He wasn't the first to be misled by my Argentinean accent acquired from my college language professor from South America.

I shook my head. *"Yo soy Americana."*

Ten minutes later, in the heart of the city, he pulled up to the address I had given. I paid the fare, slid out of the backseat, and stood on the sidewalk as the car crept away from the curb. The name of a law firm was on the building. Ricardo's office was on the second floor. My office in Long Beach was also located on the second floor of a law firm. I wondered if we shared other similarities.

To begin with, I didn't have a waiting room, let alone one large enough to comfortably fit two leather sofas and four matching chairs. I also didn't have a receptionist's desk. Or a receptionist, for that matter. The attractive brunette looked up from her work and smiled. She appeared to be in her mid-thirties.

Instinct told me the five men and the other woman in the waiting room were not a random group of clients. We were all here for the same reason.

The receptionist stood, stepped around her desk and greeted me with a friendly handshake. Speaking in Spanish, she introduced herself as Francesca Vasquez, executive secretary for *Señor* Perez. She said he would be with me momentarily and invited me to sit, gesturing to a vacant leather chair.

Three of the men were quietly talking to each other while the other two and the woman were immersed in various reading material to occupy their time. I suspected they were unaware of our mutual connection to the investigation involving Faye Franklin.

One man with a magazine stood out for his black wide-brimmed gaucho hat paired with his business suit. He had the softened jowls of someone in his sixties with a thick middle straining the buttons on his jacket.

The other three men were much younger. One was probably in his mid-twenties, very handsome with a charming smile. He wore a blue cotton t-shirt and khakis, but I received a mental image of him in a button-down shirt and tie, sitting at a desk.

In contrast, the other two men wore sport coats and slacks. The subtle definition of muscles in their necks and the broad shoulders implied their peak condition, possibly military training.

The woman appeared to be close to my age of forty-two, maybe a little younger. She was smaller, with a petite frame that seemed too fragile for the physical demands of the job I've faced. I have an athletic build suitable for scaling a chain-link fence with a Doberman on my heels.

Ten minutes later, the door beside the receptionist's desk opened, and a dark-haired gentleman walked in.

"Hello, everyone. My name is Ricardo Perez," he announced, crossing the room to the outer door. He had a pleasant but somber smile on his face as he turned the lock. "Merely a security measure, I assure you. Only to keep people out, not in."

The others glanced around with expressions that ranged from curious to confused.

"I have spoken to each of you about a missing young woman. I've gathered you together to form a team to find her. Her name is Faye Franklin. She is from the United States."

We nodded in silence.

"I believe you have already met Francesca." He raised his hand, palm up, in the direction of his secretary.

Her chin dipped as she gave him a look of respect.

He did the same.

Anyone else might misconstrue the admiration as an office romance, but I didn't get that feeling.

"I could introduce each of you individually," he said, his

open arms including the entire group. "But I prefer to let you do it yourselves. Tell us what you do and where you are from."

The cowboy spoke. "My name is Hector Diego, and I am a diplomatic liaison between Mexico and the United States. I live in Mexico City."

The casually dressed young man identified himself as José Ortega. "I am a teacher, secondary level, but I am interested in becoming an investigator. I have known Ricardo all of my life and am grateful for this opportunity to help with the case. My school is on a one-month break, and I have three weeks left that I can work investigating."

The remaining two men, Carlos Rios and Elegio Garcia, were Mexican government intelligence officers investigating the slave trade that extended beyond prostitution. Young children were also being abducted and sold, some as "orphans" to couples desperate for a child, some as house servants and others as workers in sweat-shops. They assured us other officers working similar cases would be available to assist, as needed.

Alicia Fuentes was an investigator in Corpus Christi, Texas who had worked several abduction cases. From her ease with the language, she was as comfortable speaking Spanish as I was.

After everyone finished with introductions, Ricardo spoke. "Each of you has been selected because of the skills you possess."

A soft knock at the door interrupted Ricardo, who did not appear the least bit surprised. Checking his watch, he nodded almost imperceptibly.

At the same moment, I felt a sudden change in energy. My chest tightened. My throat constricted. I recognized the sensation and knew who was on the other side of the door.

Ida Franklin.

Ricardo turned the lock and spoke English as he stepped aside to usher the middle-aged couple into the room. "This is Dr. Robert Franklin and his wife, Ida."

No surprise to me, Ida was what I like to call "a classy lady"— dark auburn hair in a sleek pageboy style, light makeup on pale skin, and wearing a light brown knee-length skirt with a matching jacket and low pumps. She was about five-six, probably around one-hundred-forty, and a good six inches shorter than her husband. He had dark hair streaked silver, particularly at his temples. His tanned face displayed character lines from years in the sun, but something told me he hadn't acquired them on a tennis court or golf course.

The doctor stepped over to Hector, shook his hand and thanked him for being there. He repeated the same greeting with each person, as did his wife.

When I saw him turn to me, I stood and introduced myself.

Ida gasped and stepped around her husband with tears in her eyes and her arms out. "I'm so grateful for what you have already done for us. It's a pleasure to finally meet you in person."

Returning her hug, I felt the burden of her worries lift a little, buoyed by renewed hope. "I only started the ball rolling to Mr. Perez. He's brought in everyone else."

Dr. Franklin said, "Modesty aside, Mrs. Acuña. You could have passed off the job and stayed in the States. We are both glad you are part of the team."

He shook my hand with a firm grip and a direct gaze that conveyed his straight-forward openness. I often assessed a lot about a person by his eye contact, or lack of it. Usually, I knew if someone was telling the truth or a lie by the way he looked at me. "Thank you, doctor."

"Please call me Robert."

I nodded. "As long as you call me Deanne, instead of Mrs. Acuña."

"You've got it." Under the circumstances, his smile was cordial but strained. He glanced at the floor, so briefly that it was hardly noticeable. Weeks of stress and sleepless nights were taking their toll. A momentary struggle with exhaustion passed as he gathered his strength and turned his attention to Ricardo. He thanked him for all that he had done, including the air and hotel arrangements.

Ricardo gripped Robert's shoulder in a show of support. "We are honored to be of service to you, sir. Please, if you have brought the items we discussed, let us get started."

"Of course."

"We brought pictures and a VHS tape of our family's Labor Day barbecue," Ida chimed in, reaching into her large handbag. She pulled out a bulging manila envelope and handed it to Ricardo.

He withdrew a handful of photos and handed them to me to pass around. I recognized a few that matched the ones I had also brought. Except for her brown hair, Faye strongly resembled her father—tall, slender, high cheekbones, strong jawline. She appeared to have the same shade of blue eyes, as well.

Speaking once again in Spanish, Ricardo asked Francesca to bring the TV and video player from his office which was not large enough to accommodate our entire group.

Francesca nodded and quietly slipped out.

Ida twisted her wedding ring as Robert recited details about their daughter as I'm sure he had already done dozens of times. "Faye is five-foot-ten and one hundred thirty-five pounds—"

"One-*twenty*-five, dear." Ida corrected with a gentle pat on his hand.

"Yes. Right. She was ... *is* an honor student, cheerleader and very active in our church and community."

"She also speaks Spanish and French extremely well. Her dream was to spend a year in Europe in a foreign studies program. Getting her passport meant more to her than getting a driver's license." Ida's voice faltered. She bowed her head, unable to say more.

Her husband slipped his arm around her and pressed a gentle kiss to the top of her head.

I was poignantly aware the Franklins were living every parent's nightmare. I sensed everyone else in the room felt the same.

Breaking the silence, Francesca opened the door and rolled an audio-visual cart into the room. A nineteen-inch television sat on the top shelf with a VHS player beneath it.

Ricardo checked his watch. "I realize some of you may have other appointments. Rather than take everyone's time by going over each person's assignment, I will meet with you individually over the next few days. If anyone needs to leave, please speak up now."

No one raised a hand.

"Very well, then." He held up the cassette cartridge that was a little larger than a paperback novel. "Now we will watch the Franklin's movies to study Faye. If her appearance has been altered in any way, she may only be recognizable by her moves, her expressions or the sound of her voice."

Ida closed her eyes briefly, her pain radiating straight to my heart.

He inserted the cassette into the player that was similar in size to an electric typewriter. The video tape ran about a half-hour, showing edited clips of various scenes featuring Faye Franklin at a family barbecue, at cheer practice, at a football game and a post-game victory party in a pizza parlor.

Halfway through, I heard soft sniffles from Ida. A few minutes later, she quietly left the office with her husband whispering to Ricardo that they would take a short walk.

I certainly understood their difficulty watching their beautiful daughter joking around with friends in the family's backyard and practicing a spirited cheer routine with her team mates. She was so full of energy and fun, surrounded by the people who loved her. I noticed one young man in the background who was particularly attentive to her, watching her with a fondness in his expression. She interacted with him like a friend, not like a romantic interest. Flirtatious but not provocative, she seemed blithely unaware of her effect on the men in her vicinity.

I couldn't help but imagine similar behavior at the club in Cancun, and another young man watching her, waiting for the opportunity to make his move.

The final clip showed Faye at the airport with her girlfriends, giddy with excitement for their adventure. Her mother's voice indicated she was behind the video camera while Faye threw her arms around her father and gave him a big kiss and hug goodbye at the gate. The last shot was the girls waving and stumbling into each other as they disappeared down the jet way.

Francesca turned up the lights, ejected the tape and handed it back to Ricardo before wheeling the cart out of the room.

We discussed Faye's general mannerisms and the possible changes to her appearance.

Ricardo placed the tape on his desk. "In my previous abduction case, the victim was heavily addicted to drugs by the time we found her. She was a shadow of her former self. Nothing like her photos. Her hair color hadn't been changed, but she was extremely thin with sunken cheeks and hollow eyes."

I was glad the Franklins had not returned to hear this conversation.

Alicia raised her hand from her lap. "If you think it would help, I could make some sketches based on Faye's picture to approximate similar changes to her facial features."

Ricardo nodded his approval. "With makeup, as well as without it."

"Of course. Do you want her to look like a cheap hooker or high-priced call-girl?"

"Both. Can you have them ready by tomorrow morning?"

"Sure thing. I'll need to borrow one of the photos."

"Francesca will make copies before you leave."

While his assistant jotted down notes at her desk, Ricardo addressed the group. "As I said earlier, I will meet with each of you individually to finalize your assignments. Francesca will set up the appointments throughout the weekend, so everyone will start work on the case no later than Monday afternoon."

CHAPTER 5

August 18, 1990
Saturday, 10:00 a.m.

After seeing the footage of Faye and hearing from Ricardo about the condition of the abducted girl he'd found, I hadn't slept well. My dreams were dark and disturbing, but nothing that could help me on this case. In the past, I received information through dreams that proved to be accurate, although not always detailed enough to lead me directly to a person or location. I was a little disappointed I hadn't received helpful guidance in last night's dream.

At sunrise, I gave up on getting any more sleep, showered, dressed and went downstairs for breakfast. I enjoyed *huevos motuleños*—eggs on tortillas with black beans and cheese. I also ordered thick, steaming *chocolate con leche* infused with cinnamon and very different from the American version of hot chocolate. But I resisted *pan de yema*, the sweet, soft bread made with lots of egg yolk and absolutely delicious when dipped into the hot chocolate. The treat was one of my favorite indulgences when Ryan and I stayed at the hotel. But I didn't need a too much food to weigh me down the rest of the day.

My meeting with Ricardo Perez was scheduled for Monday morning. I had two days to kill, which was not easy to accept. I was anxious to get started. Ten weeks had already passed since Faye had gone missing. I could only imagine how Mr. and Mrs. Franklin must have been feeling, how difficult flying back to the states had been while the rest of us searched for their daughter.

Before everyone left Ricardo's office yesterday, Francesca had asked us to return at ten-thirty this morning. For those of us without Saturday appointments, she had rented a Volkswagen bus for sight-seeing. If I hadn't read her thoughts, I would've felt visiting tourist attractions was absurd, given the unpleasant circumstances that had brought us together. She didn't tell us her underlying intention for our outing. Time together would allow us to learn about each other, to establish trust in each other. The excursion would also allow us opportunity to search the crowds for Faye.

"*Señor* Diego is not joining us?" José inquired as we followed Francesca out of the office.

Her high heels clicked on the tile. Without a pause in her stride, she turned her head and spoke over her shoulder. "He has an appointment with Ricardo at noon."

We stopped in front of the elevator and she pushed the button.

"I doubt he will be in the field like the rest of us," Carlos added while we waited for the doors to open. "Elegio and I worked with him on other cases because of his knowledge of the drug cartels—location, activities, movements."

Elegio nodded, his hands stuffed into his pockets. "Diego stays in Mexico City to keep up with daily reports from various sources so we avoid stumbling into the wrong place at the wrong time."

Alicia asked, "If he knows everything about the drug lords and their activities, why can't they be stopped?"

Elegio looked at Carlos, then back at Alicia, giving a shrug. "Informants tip them off. Officials are paid off. We are losing the battle."

"But you keep fighting it," she said with a smile of admiration.

"Once I saw the victims for the first time, I could not stop trying to help save them, even if it is only one at a time."

The elevator arrived and we filed in. The doors closed slowly. The mechanism creaked.

Carlos leaned his shoulder against the wall. "The Franklins are lucky to have the money to find their daughter. Few families are as fortunate. They can only pray for a miracle."

"Very true." Alicia made the sign of the cross with a furtive gesture to her forehead, heart and each shoulder.

José did the same, as did Francesca.

A moment later, we reached the ground floor. Francesca led us outside and up the street a short distance where the bus was parked. She handed the keys to the bus to José, who bounced them in his palm, grinning. His unique skill that brought him onto our team was his extensive knowledge of the cities and roads throughout the entire country. His father was a civil engineer who had been assigned to various locations in his career, taking along his family and providing an education in geography for José unmatched by any classroom.

As the vehicle eased into traffic, Carlos and Elegio paid no attention to the all-too-familiar history and architecture of the city. I sensed their impatience. They were eager to find the Cancun hotel where Faye had stayed and the club where she had been abducted. But Ricardo had not revealed those details during our initial meeting. Maybe he knew these young agents would be *too* eager to jump in before everyone had been given their specific assignments.

Our first stop, adjacent to the city's huge plaza, the *Zócalo*, was the *Catedral Metropolitana*—the oldest and largest cathedral in Latin America. We skipped the tour but stayed together with José as our guide.

Alicia and I struck up a conversation about our investigative work and bonded immediately. Her previous career as a professional makeup artist in film and television made her an expert with disguises, a strong asset for undercover work. Leaving Hollywood for a career as a federal investigator for the United States government, she retired a couple of years ago and now worked human trafficking cases.

"Ricardo introduced himself at the C.I.I. conference in June," she explained. "Apparently, my background in theatrical makeup impressed him. That, and my Spanish."

"After seeing your sketches of Faye, I can understand why Ricardo brought you into the assignment. You're a talented artist."

"Thanks, Deanne. I appreciate that."

"Something tells me you have really good instincts, too."

She laughed. "It's that female intuition. Comes in handy in our business, don't you think?"

"Definitely."

When we talked about his reasons for picking each one of

us, I could "hear" Alicia's curiosity about me. Like her, I am one of a small number of women with a certification for international investigations. Like her, I speak Spanish. But she couldn't figure out the skill I brought to the team.

As we walked, I discretely kept my eye on the man I'd noticed who had been shadowing us most of the day. I sensed him there, sensed too that he wasn't a danger. Perhaps a security measure Richard had put in place.

I looked back at Alicia. "Mr. and Mrs. Franklin," I explained without being asked, "came to me through a referral. When another investigator couldn't take their case, he told them about my success with locating people who were difficult to find."

"So, you're the one who brought them to Ricardo."

"Yes. I knew I couldn't tackle this case alone. I needed someone here in Mexico who knows his own country better than I do."

"I would've done the same."

CHAPTER 6

August 20, 1990
Monday, 8:00 a.m.

During our two days together, the five of us traveled around the city, ate meals together and drank *cerveza* in the bar of my hotel. Alicia and I realized we shared the same appointment time with Ricardo, so we arranged to meet for breakfast and take a taxi together to his office.

"Buenos días, señoras," Francesca greeted as we entered the reception area.

We followed her into a hallway, passing two closed doors before reaching Ricardo's office. She knocked quietly on the opaque glass, opened the door, told him we had arrived, then stepped back to let us pass.

The large room was sparsely furnished with modern chrome and glass furniture. The space was also impeccably neat and clean, much like the man himself. The glass-top desk held a large open notebook he had been reading.

He smiled and rose to his feet as we entered and extended his hand. *"Bienvenido. ¿Cómo estás?"*

"Bienvenido, Señor Perez. Muy bien, gracias." Alicia shook his hand.

"Ricardo, *por favor.*"

She smiled. "Ricardo."

He turned to me and shook my hand. "Please, take a seat."

Alicia and I sat in the two chairs opposite his desk as he returned to his own seat and settled back. "Your assignment is to pretend you have just opened a store in Los Angeles and you are seeking handmade items to purchase throughout Mexico, Central America and South America. This will give you access to small towns."

"I already have a fictitious boutique called 'Sophie's Treasures'," I said. "It was set up as my cover investigating trademark infringement in the L.A. garment district."

"Excellent." He nodded.

"I doubt anyone will ask for proof that we are legitimate business owners," Alicia said, "but it's smart to have something in place."

Ricardo said, "It would *not* be smart for two women to travel alone. José will be going along as your driver. For added safety, Mr. and Mrs. Franklin have allowed me to hire a retired police officer to shadow you."

Ricardo caught my smile and stopped.

The corner of his mouth turned up as a realization dawned. "You were aware of him, yes?"

I nodded. "Six-one. Around a hundred-eighty. Dark brown hair and eyes. About fifty."

"Yes, that sounds like him."

"He's very good at what he does. None of the others knew he was following us."

Alicia gawked, her eyes wide. "Are you kidding me? We had a tail, and you are the only one who spotted him?"

"Not until Saturday evening," I answered. Even though I had sensed his presence shortly after we'd started our tour of the city in the morning, I hadn't felt the need to explain my intuitive abilities yet.

"Yes," Ricardo confirmed, "He has been with you for the past two days."

"Is that Pete?"

"How did you know?"

I shrugged. "Lucky guess."

With a shake of her head, Alicia pointed at me. "You invited him over to our table in the bar last night."

"Yes," I admitted.

"I thought he was only flirting with you. That same guy was on us all weekend? I'm surprised Carlos and Elegio didn't pick up on him."

Despite the fact the two agents hadn't realized Pete had tailed us, they were definitely guarded when I invited him to our table. He'd introduced himself as Pete Young from Miami, Florida. I hadn't needed to be psychic to have already figured out he was, or had been, in law enforcement. The fact that he'd been following us was evidence enough.

"Pete has worked for me on several cases in the states," Ricardo explained. "I would trust him with my own life."

Alicia said, "That's good enough for me."

I spoke up. "Ricardo, I've been thinking about bringing in a young woman from L.A. She's worked in some nightclubs in Los Angeles that have suspected ties to the Mexican Mafia. She understands how the clubs operate, and I believe she could be a great help."

His eyes narrowed. "Have you discussed this case with her?"

"Only in generalities. Client confidentiality is important to me."

"What is your connection to her?"

"She's working under my license until she gets her own."

I wasn't privileged to tell him I'd met Sandy when she was living with an abusive boyfriend. Another investigator and I had helped her to escape and relocate to Portland, Oregon. After her ex ended up in prison for the brutal murder of a twenty-three-year-old woman, Sandy returned to L.A., taking a job with a temp agency for the flexible schedule. The rest of the time she worked on accumulating the six thousand hours of experience required for a private investigator license.

Ricardo tapped his pen on his desk pad, thinking. A moment later, he looked up at me. "If you think she is worth waiting for her to get here, call her." He picked up the dial phone on his desk and turned it around to face me.

I dug in my bag for my notebook with contact numbers, found hers and dialed it.

As it rang, Alicia asked, "I hope she already has a passport."

"She does," I answered, recalling a conversation about a trip to Australia with her boyfriend that had been cancelled at the last minute, through no fault of hers. But she'd suffered the brunt of his anger anyway.

Sandy answered on the sixth ring, breathless from running to catch the phone. "Is everything okay?" she asked after we'd said our hellos.

"Yes, everything is fine. I'm sorry to give you such short

notice but—"

"Am I being fired?"

I chuckled. "How could I fire you when you're the best apprentice I've ever had?"

"I'm the *only* apprentice you've ever had."

From her tone, I knew she was smiling. "I'm calling to say I need you in Mexico."

"Really? Wow! Cool!"

I covered the phone and looked at Ricardo. "She says yes."

Ricardo raised an eyebrow, "I didn't hear you ask her."

"No need." I turned my attention back to Sandy. "We'll be posing as shop owners buying merchandise for our store. I need you to bring my file labeled 'Sophie's Treasures' with the seller's permit and the IRS letter with the Employee Identification number."

"Originals or copies?"

"Originals."

"Then I'll guard them with my life."

I grinned. "Good. Ask Kitty to book your plane ticket. Pack light—two changes of clothes and toiletries. Don't forget your passport."

《—》

Back in my hotel room an hour later, I called Ryan at his shop. He answered in his professional voice that softened after he realized I was on the line. I told him about the weekend with my team members, but none of the details of our plans. I also told him I was hoping to be home in two weeks.

"Just hoping, huh? Nothing definite?"

"Sorry, no."

"I suppose I should be grateful that you aren't sharing any details, but I'm not."

"Don't worry, we have a good team. I promise to call you every other day if I can get service. Sandy is coming down in a couple days, too."

"I'd make a better bodyguard."

"Nice try. I have a different job in mind for her. And somehow, I don't think the average guy in a nightclub will find you as attractive in a miniskirt."

"I don't know about that. I have pretty good lookin' legs."

I laughed. "I know. Everything about you is a pretty good looking."

"If I wasn't sitting here in my office where anybody could walk in on me ...."

His comment trailed off, leaving me to read his intimate thoughts. "You're making me blush."

He chuckled. "If only I had your talent for telepathy."

"Seems to me you're doing fine right now. Our minds are definitely on the same track."

We talked for ten more minutes before Ryan had to answer another call and reluctantly said good-bye.

CHAPTER 7

August 22, 1990
Wednesday, 7:15 a.m.

The earliest direct flight was Wednesday at four in the morning, bringing Sandy into Mexico City International airport long before breakfast. José drove Ricardo and me to pick her up in Ricardo's black Buick sedan. She came out of the jet way wearing cowboy boots, jeans and a light jacket over an open button-shirt on top of a t-shirt. Definitely over-dressed for the hot August heat, she knew how to travel with extra clothes on her back that wouldn't fit into the carry-on suitcase she held in one hand. In the other hand was a small backpack in lieu of a purse.

I waved to gain her attention.

She grinned and waved back, heading our direction. She had cropped her long black hair since I'd last seen her. The ponytail was gone. The pixie-short style was brushed forward.

"Hi, Deanne!" She gave me a hug. "Like my new look?"

"It's perfect on you."

"After I saw 'Ghost' a couple weeks ago, I went right out and got it cut just like Demi Moore's." Switching her backpack to the hand carrying her bag, she reached out to Ricardo, speaking in Spanish. "Hi, I'm Sandy Carter, but friends call me

Sandy."

"Welcome, Sandy." Ricardo returned the handshake. "My name is Ricardo Perez—"

"So, you're the head honcho, huh?"

He smiled and gave a slight bow. "I am."

"Cool," she said in English, then turned to our driver and offered her hand, returning to Spanish. "Hi, I'm Sandy and you are?"

"José Ortega. *Yo tengo mucho gusto conocerle.*" *I have great pleasure to meet you.* Instead of shaking her hand, he lifted it and lightly kissed the back. "I also speak English, if you are more comfortable with that."

From her slow blinks to her gaped mouth, she looked star-struck. "G-great. My Spanish is awful."

Seeing the way they gazed at each other, I was immediately aware of the attraction between the two. I also recognized their mutual interest could work in our favor.

Ricardo waited until we were in the car before he would talk about the investigation. Considering the never-ending traffic jam, we weren't getting back to his office very soon. An eighteen-minute drive could take us thirty.

Sandy, who had taken the passenger seat across from José, twisted around to look at Ricardo as he talked.

"Deanne said you are familiar with the clubs that might have ties to drug cartels."

"My ex-boyfriend and I hung out at them a lot in L.A. He bragged he knew the Mexicans running those places."

"Do you think he was telling the truth?"

"Yeah. Sorta. Not like he was best buds with them, or

anything like that. They might have done some business with each other in the past. Maybe still were, but I never saw it."

"Did you see prostitutes in these bars?" Ricardo asked.

"Hard to miss. My ex liked to tell me that I'd better be good to him or he'd replace me with one of those girls. They're a dime a dozen, he said. Most of them didn't speak a word of English."

"They were probably brought across the border illegally," José interjected.

"No surprise there," Sandy answered. "No papers. No skills. No English. No way home."

I added, "Human trafficking is getting worse every year."

"So, do I get to do anything? Or am I just along for the ride?" she joked, her gaze flicking between the back-seat passengers.

"You know the club scene," I answered. "You'd fit right in."

"As bait?" Not waiting for a response, she threw her head back and laughed. "That's too funny!"

Our silence stopped her. She looked at each one of us.

"Seriously? Holy crap. Me?"

I scooted forward in my seat. "I told Ricardo that you would be a great team member because you know the club scene. You also have really good instincts, Sandy. Putting you inside makes sense to see if we can lure the man who took Faye. You're young. Attractive. Those people will be looking for an opportunity to drug you so they can get you out of the club easily."

She gazed at me intently. "Nothing like jumping into the

deep end on my first real gig, huh?"

"Stay alert. Stay focused and you'll do okay." Even though I'd worked other cases of human trafficking for labor, none involved kidnapping. Anyone with any common sense knew we were entering dangerous territory. But my gut instinct told me we'd all be okay, including Sandy. Circumstances could change, of course. At the moment, intuitively, I wasn't getting the feeling of imminent danger, only caution.

"If you don't mind my asking, why are we in Mexico City when Faye disappeared in Cancun? Shouldn't we start by looking into the bar where she was last seen?"

Ricardo shook his head. "As I had told Deanne, the kidnappers move their victims immediately out of the area so they cannot easily find their way back if they escape. We could scour Cancun but she will be long gone by now. Another city. Possibly another country."

Sandy worried her lower lip. "I've heard rumors at the L.A. clubs but never thought I would be involved in a case that could get me kidnapped."

"You will be surrounded by others who are capable of protecting you."

She turned to José. "You're my body guard?"

"Yes. No. Actually, I am a teacher."

"You're pulling my leg, right?"

He shook his head.

"How does a teacher end up a chauffeur-slash-bodyguard?"

"I have admired Ricardo since I was a little boy. Always asking him about his cases. My parents encouraged me to pursue a safer, more reliable vocation. I love being a teacher and I can always go back to it, but I want to explore the possibility of becoming an investigator."

Ricardo stated, "Now that Sandy is here, you can leave for Cuernavaca as soon as possible. The man who was with Faye Franklin at the club in Cancun has been identified through the photo provided by her parents. He's James Krieger from a wealthy family in Germany. He speaks several languages and is a member of a group of men who own clubs in Mexico, Central and South America."

Sandy's eyes widened. "The Mexican Mafia?"

He shook his head. "What you call 'Mexican Mafia' was started by Chicano gang members in California. They are just vendors for the Mexican drug cartels who moved up from trafficking cocaine for the Columbians."

Sandy studied him. "Are you saying Faye Franklin was kidnapped over drugs?"

"No. The cartels have their fingers in every criminal venture—kidnapping, prostitution, money-laundering, human trafficking. The disappearance of the Franklin girl has all the signs of abduction for the sex trade."

"So, Krieger is involved in one of these cartels?" I asked.

"Possibly, yes. He *is* one of the main players with these clubs. Unfortunately, there were no reports of a young, American woman being seen at any of their clubs north of Mexico City, according to our sources. We have no one to report from the southern clubs. That is why you will go to Cuernavaca."

"Is Kreiger there?"

Ricardo answered, "As far as I know, he is still in Cancun.

But your job is to find Franklin, not Kreiger."

Ricardo and José dropped us off at my hotel, then Sandy showered and changed into something more suitable for the heat—a tank top, shorts and sandals. She tied the jacket around her waist since there was no room for it in either of the bags. After she closed her suitcase, she slid a thin leather belt through the bootstraps of her well-worn cowboy boots and hung them from each side of the bag. We checked out and grabbed a bite to eat in the hotel's restaurant before meeting everyone at Ricardo's office.

Our new transportation was a faded-brown, older-model Dodge B-350 panel van with three wide wrap-around graphic stripes in burnt orange, cream and coffee. It had definitely seen better days. The passenger side had an opaque tinted window. Close to the rear of the van was another tinted window—tall, wide with a vent along the bottom. The same size windows were also on the driver's side. Thankfully, the van had a rooftop air conditioner.

"Wait until you see the inside." José waved a dismissive hand at the outside. He'd already spent a full day with the technician who had installed specialized equipment.

He slid open the side door to reveal the custom conversion with carpet, cabinets, and the smallest sink I'd ever seen. A bench seat next to the back windows converted into a bed. A table could also be transformed into a bed, according to José. I didn't know how it would fit without blocking the small refrigerator in a cabinet next to the sliding door.

"We also have two satellite telephones, a television, two tracking devices, a camera and ..." He stepped up inside and moved to the back of the van.

Alicia chuckled. "He's like a kid in a candy store."

José returned with a white plastic case and placing it on the table in front of us. "A new Compaq SLT/286 laptop computer with 40-megabyte hard disk drive that is shock-mounted so it won't be affected by rough roads." He opened the case and pointed at the machine. "It runs on a battery for three hours and it only weighs fourteen pounds! The keyboard even detaches. We have a printer, too. Isn't this great?"

Clearly, he was thrilled with his newest gadget. I, on the other hand, hadn't yet warmed up to the idea of computers. I still preferred my Smith-Corona.

Ricardo clapped his hands once. "Are you ready to start, my friends?"

"Yes," we said in unison.

"Remember to stay near Sandy at all times. Pete will be following in his white Bronco. He'll maintain enough distance to keep anyone from connecting your two vehicles. Allow him to be the one to approach you when he knows conditions are safe. Now stow your bags and get started. I'll stay in touch with Deanne and José."

CHAPTER 8

August 22, 1990
Wednesday, 10:45 a.m.

Ten minutes later, we were on our way to Cuernavaca, forty-five miles southeast of Mexico City.

Alicia and I sat on the bench seat, allowing Sandy to ride shotgun in front.

She was full of energy, keyed up with the excitement of embarking on a thrilling adventure. Pointing at places and things along our route, she asked José a million and one questions, which he seemed tireless to answer.

The road out of the city was crowded with vehicles and vendors, as usual.

I leaned forward to open the refrigerator, pleased to find it fully stocked. "Would any of you like something cold to drink?"

They all requested Coca-Cola. I handed two cans to Sandy. She took them, popped them open and handed one to José. He smiled wide and thanked her. She smiled back. I glanced at Alicia observing the exchange. She saw me watching her and shrugged with an amused expression.

Sandy twisted around in her seat to speak to Alicia and me. "Have either of you worked a kidnapping case before?"

Alicia nodded. "But the kidnapper was the father in a child custody case in California. Nothing like this."

"I've investigated human trafficking," I answered. "Workers in the garment district in Los Angeles and on farms in Central California. They were smuggled across the border with the promise of good jobs. But they end up working long hours for well below the minimum wage."

Sandy's smile faded. "I suppose it's still better than what they'd make in their own country, huh?"

I sighed, remembering so many disheartened faces of the illegal immigrants. "Even though the pay is low, they have nothing better at home. Most have limited education or none at all because they have no money to pay for it. Most workers send some of their paychecks to family back home, never knowing if they will ever see them again."

Sandy dropped her gaze to the floor.

I knew she was comparing the struggles in her own past, leaving her family behind to escape her abusive boyfriend. But she was not ready to talk about it in front of Alicia and José.

She swallowed hard. Before turning back around, she glanced at me, aware of my ability to pick up thoughts projected by strong emotions.

Her gaze acknowledged my perception of her momentary lapse into her painful past. In a single look, I felt a warm glow in my heart. Love. Appreciation. She did not yet know how to actually read minds, but she had learned how to send and perceive emotional energy.

Sandy settled into her seat, looking out the windshield.

《—》

An hour later, we finally traveled at a speed greater than five miles per hour, though not by much. José told us our destination of Cuernavaca had grown considerably in recent years because of its close proximity to Mexico City and its popularity worldwide as a vacation spot. Many people were buying affordable homes in the lush valley and commuting to the larger metropolis. The narrow, two-lane Highway 95 could no longer bear the burden of so many vehicles. A new eight-lane highway had been started three years earlier but was still years away from completion.

Our route led us into the mountainous areas of the Yoyolica volcano, leaving behind the threatening gloom of rain clouds. José often swerved around large potholes, apologizing whenever he hadn't been quick enough to see one in time before we were bounced in our seats.

We passed through tiny towns and dense pine and oak forests, reaching the highest elevation of nearly ten thousand feet as we crossed from the Federal District into the tiny state of Morelos. From Huitzilac, we drove into the most harrowing section of highway with twists and turns, dropping down into the "land of eternal spring." Unfortunately, our view was obscured by a layer of smoke from a farmer's burn-off.

Although, I suspected some of the brown haze could be attributed to the smog from the cars. In the states, we might have traveled the same distance in less than an hour. Instead, we arrived three hours after we'd left Mexico City.

José tuned the radio to a local music station where a disc

jockey announced that Cuernavaca was experiencing an unusual record-breaking heat wave with temperatures expected to reach the low nineties by late afternoon. He drove to the historic center of town where Ricardo's assistant, Francesca, had reserved rooms in a first-class hotel, more for our safety than for the luxury. Although this was a resort town, there were still the seedier areas to contend with.

On our way to our rooms to relax for a couple hours before dinner, I recognized Pete walking into the hotel. As per our instructions, we didn't acknowledge him, or he us.

Alicia, Sandy and I shared one room with two double beds and a rollaway. It was a little crowded but doable. José made sure everything was okay, then left to go to his room next to ours.

Sandy dropped her things on the portable bed and stretched, raising her arms over her head and bending side to side. "I don't know about you two but I've been sitting for too long. Think I can go to the pool for a couple hours?"

Alicia glanced at me, concern in her gaze.

I shook my head. "Unfortunately, Sandy, this isn't L.A. You heard Ricardo. I'm afraid you can't go anywhere alone. It's too risky."

She swept her arms outward. "Even here in this fancy place? What could happen to me here? Aren't we supposed to be acting like normal people on a buying trip?"

"This is not a vacation, Sandy. We can't let down our guard. I'm sorry."

"What if José came with me?" She tucked one leg behind the other and sat on the bed.

"He's had a very long day of driving. Let him have a *siesta*. If you want to take a walk around the hotel, I'll go with you."

"Are you sure you don't mind?"

"Not at all. You're right about sitting for so long. I need a little exercise to get the blood flowing." I turned to Alicia. "You're welcome to join us."

"Go ahead," she said, waving us out the door. "I'm in the mood for a short nap."

I checked my watch. "We'll be back in an hour."

When we returned, I opened our door and stepped on a piece of paper on the floor. Apparently, Alicia had been sleeping when José decided to go out to the craft markets to make arrangements for us to meet with local vendors. His note informed us he would be back to take us to dinner at a nearby restaurant.

«—»

Later, leaving the van safely parked at the hotel, the four of us walked a few blocks to a sidewalk café across from one of the nightclubs we wanted to check out. The hour was too early for the real action of the evening, but we chose a table positioned to view an alley leading to the back entrance.

During our meal, we talked about the shopping excursion ahead, avoiding the true topic of our assignment where we could be overheard. We kept our eyes and ears open, even though the previous report had indicated Faye Franklin might have been taken to another country.

I wish my intuition sensed she was close by. But I wasn't picking up anything. Sometimes, I don't even realize until afterward that I've been guided to a specific place for a reason. In the meantime, I rely on the same investigative techniques as any other flatfoot, trusting I will be in the right place at the right time.

José and Sandy sat with their backs to the street so Alicia and I could talk to them while watching the delivery trucks come and go at the club.

At one point, my attention was drawn away from the others at the table. I looked down the sidewalk at people smiling and greeting each other in passing. Nothing stood out, and yet, I sensed ... something. I thought about Pete and wondered if I was simply feeling his presence nearby in the shadows. I knew he was out there somewhere, keeping us under his protective surveillance.

No, the cause of my unease wasn't him. I can't explain how I knew. I just had a faint notion that a storm, of sorts, was brewing. The question was what and when.

CHAPTER 9

August 23, 1990
Thursday, 8:00 a.m.

Our first stop of the morning would be the *Mercado de Artesanias y Plata*—Market of Craft and Silver—next to the Palace of Cortes. To move freely about the country without suspicion, we had to act as the boutique owners on a buying trip. José pointed out sights as he maneuvered the streets as if he was a year-round resident.

"Did your family live here when you were young?" I asked.

He chuckled. "It is obvious, yes?"

"Yes, it is. You automatically turn down another street if the road is congested."

He grinned, pulling back his shoulders proudly. "I learned to drive here. I only wish we had more time so I could show you all of the wonderful gardens and museums. Maybe you will come back again after our work is done?"

I knew he was speaking more to Sandy than to Alicia and me. "I have very dear friends who live in Mexico. On my next visit, if Sandy is available, I could bring her with me."

Sandy lit up. "Really, Deanne? You'd do that? I'd so love to come back!"

José pulled the van over to the curb beneath an imposing

monument of General Carlos Pacheco Villalobos in front of the palace. "The only parking is a block away so I will drop you here. You have a meeting in ten minutes with a vendor of hammocks and pottery made by local artists. *Señor* Garcia is in stall number fifteen to your right. I will meet you in thirty minutes."

The market was full of shoppers—some lingering at the overflowing display tables, some bustling by with their purchases. We made our way slowly past stalls of handmade clothing, blankets, papier-mâché figures, wood-carved animals, and silver jewelry.

The shop owner waited in front of his stall. He didn't look much older than Sandy.

"¡Hola, senoritas!"

Alicia and I laughed at his audacious flattery to address all of us as young ladies, not just Sandy.

I shook his hand with a smile and a wink. "Thank you, kind sir."

Acting as store-owners ourselves, we chatted about our thriving new business in Los Angeles and our excitement about adding more hand-crafted items to our inventory. We shared about our current buying trip that was taking us to numerous regions of Mexico. Fortunately, Alicia and I had enough knowledge from our previous travels so that we could carry on a convincing conversation about our purchases in other towns.

Shortly before we needed to leave to meet back with José, we ordered twenty hammocks from Mr. Garcia which made him extremely happy. I gave him the shipping address of the Santa Monica boutique owned by a former client who had agreed to help. I needed a location where someone would be available to sign for deliveries and the space to store them until I returned. Maxine had already expressed interest in acquiring some, if not all, of our purchases for her store. After the assignment was over, we would figure out what to do with the merchandise.

As Mr. Garcia stood by while I signed the credit card slip, he thanked us again and again. In all his years as a merchant, he'd never made such a large sale. He was looking forward to celebrating with his wife and children.

"I hope my hammocks will sell well so you will contact me for more," he said, pressing his business card into my palm.

"I do, too." I felt guilty for his optimistic plans of future transactions. But I was glad our visit today had been so profitable for him.

When we returned to the street, we saw the brown van pull up to the curb by the statue. The three of us hurried to get in before another car went by.

"How did it go?" José asked as we settled into our seats.

"*Señor* Garcia was a real treasure to meet. He was very grateful to you for the business and wants to express his appreciation. So he wants you to come by and pick out something for yourself next time you are in town."

"Did he tell you his father-in-law is the mayor of Cuernavaca?"

"No, he didn't talk about himself," Alicia answered, "just his wife and his two young daughters."

Sandy sighed heavily. "I don't understand. I thought we had an appointment with Señor Garcia because he could help us find Faye. All we did was buy stuff."

"We must do everything to maintain our cover as shop owners," I answered. "If we are stopped by law enforcement or suspicious cartel members, we need receipts and shipping invoices. We need to interact with sellers who can honestly corroborate our reason for being in each town."

Alicia added, "Real life investigating is nothing like you see on TV or the movies. Hollywood whitewashes the tedious, often unproductive hours of work. Trust me, setting up a cover and maintaining it seems like a waste of time but we must take every precaution to avoid detection of our real purpose for being here."

Sandy slowly nodded. "I still have a lot to learn."

I patted her shoulder. "You're doing fine. Just keep asking questions."

I turned to José, "Have you been in touch with Ricardo?"

He glanced in the rearview mirror and met my gaze with wide-eyed surprise. "As a matter of fact, I called him while I was gone. Apparently, those two government agents we met in Ricardo's office have informants who have given them reason to believe we are wasting our time here in Cuernavaca. The club we were going to check out tonight changed hands a few days ago. The new owner is clean."

"For now, anyway." I couldn't help but remember the strange feeling I'd felt at the restaurant. Maybe there was trouble ahead for the new owner.

"Aren't there other clubs in town?" Sandy asked.

José shrugged. "Yes, but I am only doing as I am told. I do not ask questions."

"How long do you think we will we be in Acapulco?"

"Two or three days, depending on what we learn. Ricardo has sent Carlos and Elegio ahead to do their part of the investigation."

"And?" I had the feeling he knew something he wasn't telling us yet.

"Deanne, I can't hide anything from you, can I? There are two new girls working at a popular club in Acapulco. Neither of them matches the photos of Faye Franklin. Ricardo thought they might know something, and that they might talk to Sandy if she can get friendly with them."

Sandy fidgeted.

"You'll do fine," I assured her.

Alicia reached into her purse and brought out an ornamental broach. "I think we're going to need this."

Sandy squinted to see what she was holding. "A lapel pin? Why?"

"It's a hidden camera. Hopefully, we can get IDs from the photographs."

"Oh, wow!" Sandy lit up, forgetting her anxiety. "That is so awesome! Just like in the movies."

"I used to think so, too," Alicia answered. "The gadgets are great, of course. But we're not on a Hollywood back lot and the bad guys aren't actors. If the two girls know anything about Faye and they're caught talking about her, all three of you could be killed."

A gasp sounded. "Killed?" Sandy snapped her fingers. "Just like that?"

I nodded. "*If* Faye has been kidnapped by these people, and *if* she's identified, they will look at her as a liability. Same for the other two. They'd be disposed of before anyone could do anything about it."

Blinking hard, Sandy cupped her hand over her mouth, turned back around in her seat and didn't say another word for a long time.

«—»

The seven-hour drive to Acapulco along Highway 95 left us drained. We'd encountered every obstacle imaginable, short of a washed-out bridge—twists, turns, bumps, potholes, stalled cars, slow-moving donkey carts and cows standing in the road.

Entering the northern end of the city in the late afternoon also slowed our progress to Revolcadero Beach. Turning onto Simon Bolívar, we entered the grounds of the Princess Hotel with a lush green golf course on both sides of the street.

Sandy stared slack-jawed at the fifteen-story modern-day Aztec pyramid rising into the blue sky. Colorful flowers spilled from the terraced balconies across the entire façade. "Deanne, you'll have to remind me we're not on vacation," she said. "We're staying here?"

"Ricardo really knows how to pick the hotels." Alicia smiled, gazing across the street at the expanse of green grass.

José boasted, "Actually, I am the one who booked the hotel this time. Ricardo asked me to find one with the best security. Tomorrow, we'll go to the shops and tomorrow night, we'll go to our first club."

He followed the circular drive and stopped in front of the open-air lobby, and an eager valet hurried to the driver's door.

José shook his head. "I am only dropping off my clients," he said while Sandy, Alicia and I climbed out with our bags.

The man kept his smile firmly in place, even though he was disappointed to lose the tip for parking the van. I knew from my own travels in Mexico that the average worker in the tourist industry relied heavily on gratuities to supplement their very low wages. For some, tips were their only source of income.

José reached through his window with a folded bill. *"Le agradecería si usted pudiera mostrarme dónde aparcar."*

"Sí." The valet perked up, taking the cash and giving directions to the self-parking area. Stepping back, he held up the money. *"Muchas gracias."*

CHAPTER 10

August 24, 1990
Friday, 9:50 a.m.

Planning for our late night at the club, we slept an hour longer and ate a later breakfast before starting out on our shopping excursion. José kept us on a tight schedule, playing his role of tour guide as he escorted us from market to market, stall to stall. All of the shop owners were familiar with him and clearly liked him.

"This doesn't appear to be the first time you've brought tourists to these markets," Alicia said while we were en route to our second stop of the day.

"When I needed money for school, I gave private tours and realized how much the shop owners depend on guides to bring in customers. After I started teaching, I didn't need the money but I missed the people so I came back to it during my holidays until a couple years ago."

"Is it common for them to tip you?" Sandy asked.

He shrugged. "It is not the same as tipping a waitress for good service. The merchants look at it as sharing the profit of the sale like a business partnership. If I'd refused, I would have made them suspicious."

I thought to myself that he had been a good choice for our

guide. "That was a smart decision, José."

"I'll be happy to turn everything over to you at the end of the day, Deanne. I don't think keeping it would be right."

Sandy raised her hand. "You could treat us to dinner tonight."

I shook my head. She had a lot to learn about the business. "We need to account for everything in the expense report for the Franklins, including dinners. In the end, I don't want any question about cash going out or coming in. I'll log the tips in my ledger and give you a receipt, José."

He nodded. "That is fine with me."

The rest of the morning and afternoon passed quickly. We purchased hand-painted pottery, embroidered clothing, colorful tablecloths with napkins, small woven rugs and silver jewelry. Everything had to be shipped, even the smallest items. Aside from the lack of space in the van, José warned us tourists are easy targets for robbery. Thieves loitered around the markets, watching anyone buying jewelry or expensive souvenirs that could be pawned or resold on the black market.

At three-thirty, on the way back to our hotel, José mentioned we needed to wear dresses to get into the club.

"You're telling us that now?" Alicia held up her hands, palms up. "I packed only the bare essentials."

"Me, too," I said.

With a shake of her head, Sandy added, "I didn't even bring a simple sundress."

I'd known we would need to purchase suitable nightclub attire for Sandy but hadn't considered the need for Alicia or myself.

José smiled. "There is a shop in the hotel that should have a good selection for all of you."

"I bet you've already told the owner we would be stopping by. Am I right?" One corner of Alicia's mouth lifted.

"Yes, you are. And she tips very generously. So, spend a lot of *pesos*."

《—》

At eight p.m., José knocked on our door. "Are you ready?"

"All set," I answered as I greeted him with a sweep of my hand to show the new dress. Alicia and I had chosen simple sleeveless sheaths that would be easy to clean and pack. Mine was black, hers was a deep teal.

"You look very nice." José nodded his approval, stepping aside to let me pass. Alicia followed. "You, too."

Wearing a sly smile, she winked at him. "Wait till you see Sandy."

Sandy walked into view wearing a short, red mini-dress in a body-hugging knit fabric with an off-the-shoulder neckline. She'd wanted to go with a Madonna-inspired outfit that included huge hoop earrings, chunky heels, a bustier, leather jacket and matching mini. Since luggage space was an issue, she'd compromised by getting the earrings to go with the wrinkle-free knit dress and strappy stilettos. Her short black hair was gelled into a shiny tousled style.

José was speechless as Alicia had predicted. He didn't find his voice until we reached the lobby when he explained he would hail a taxi so the van would remain safe and secure at the hotel.

Arriving at the club early allowed us to get an idea of the room layout before the place was crowded. José paid the cover charge for our group of four, and we passed two large security men dressed in suits and acting as doormen.

The maître d' eyed us with aloof dismissal until Sandy stepped out from behind us and smiled flirtatiously. Suddenly, he became a bit too interested. My skin crawled from the mental imagery he projected.

José moved in between them, slipping cash to the man while explaining he was our tour guide and we three ladies were American tourists who wanted to see a high-class nightclub.

The maître d' discreetly checked the currency before it disappeared into his pocket and escorted us to the back of the room.

Leaning close, I whispered to Sandy, "Tell him you want to be closer to the bar and dance floor."

She gave me a wink and a nod. With little persuasion, she had the man leading us to a booth with a clear view of the bar.

Alicia slid in one side and scooted around the curved bench to the back of the table, giving herself a good vantage point for taking photographs with her hidden camera. I sat next to her. As planned, Sandy and José took each end, opposite each other so they would not be mistaken as a couple. Sandy had to appear available to men who might want her to dance.

By ten p.m., the club was full and the air was thick with cigarette smoke, stinging my eyes and burning my throat. The female singer in the band looked a lot like Whitney Houston and sounded pretty close to the real singer. No one seemed to notice or care as long as they could dance to the music.

Sandy accepted invitations to dance, and José selected his own partners so he would also appear single and looking for some action.

Alicia and I nursed watered-down drinks and studied any young woman who looked unattached. Sometimes, a man would approach one of them holding two cocktails, indicating they were a couple—at least for that night. Other times, a potentially single young woman would be joined by girlfriends who had just arrived.

Every so often, a girl would lead a gentleman down a hall beyond the bar. Eventually, we narrowed the field to the women lingering around the male patrons at the bar. Some of the girls wore flashy costume jewelry. A few flaunted tastefully elegant diamond earrings and tennis bracelets that told me they were probably well-kept trophy wives or mistresses seeking a cheap thrill. Their expensive accessories elevated them above the category of girls we were looking for.

The female singer finished a Madonna song and announced the next number would be sung by their lead guitarist, Acapulco's version of rapper Tone-Lōc.

He stepped up to the microphone as the drummer started a heavy bass beat. "Hey, girls, you ready to do the nasty?" he yelled. The crowded cheered. "Let's do it." He launched into a song about doing the wild thing.

Several of the single girls we'd been watching led their prospective clients to the floor and began a rhythmic bump and grind to the sexually explicit lyrics.

At the bar, a blonde stood by a man sitting on a stool, her

body leaning into him and swaying to the beat. His back was to us, his hand on her thigh, sliding up her short skirt. She nuzzled his ear but her disinterested gaze kept staring toward our table.

He swiveled his seat a quarter-turn and moved her between his legs, pulling her hips against his groin and kissing her neck.

She tilted her head back as if she was in ecstasy. But, again, her gaze turned back toward us.

I sensed her fear. Desperation. Defiance. Her emotions transmitted so strong that I felt my own excitement escalate about the connection. I hoped this was a potentially positive step in the investigation.

"José, don't look right now but there's a woman in a yellow top at the bar," I said. "She's been glancing over here, and I'm wondering if she might know you."

He waited a couple of minutes before he let his gaze casually sweep the room and turn back to me. "I have never seen her before tonight."

"I'll go to the restroom. Watch her and see what happens."

Now the guitarist singer channeled Bruce Springsteen. I grabbed my purse, slid out of the booth and walked past the bar, following the signs toward the restrooms. I entered the same hallway where the girls had taken their clients. After I went into a stall, I heard the click of heels on the tile floor.

Someone entered the stall next to mine.

I recognized the silver t-strap heels. I finished my business and walked to the counter of wash basins.

The girl in the yellow top stepped up to the sink beside me. We both looked in the mirror and exchanged a polite smile.

I greeted, *"Hola. ¿Cómo estás?"* Hi. How are you?

Her return smile faded. *"¿Usted no es un Americano?"* You are not an American?

My Argentinean accent had surprised and disappointed her. I also noticed she didn't speak the language effortlessly as a native. *"Sí. Soy Americano."*

Her expression brightened. "You don't sound like one," she said with the slightest Southern drawl.

"My dialect fools everyone."

As she dried her hands, she flicked her glance at the closed door and back.

I could feel her distress even stronger now. "Are you in trouble?" I asked. "Do you need help? I can help you."

Fear flashed in her eyes and her hands shook slightly. "It's too hard to explain here. Can I meet you somewhere tomorrow morning? I must work until the club closes in the morning." She tugged at her clothes, nervously licking her lips. "But me and the other girls are allowed to go wherever we want during the day. Within a reasonable distance, that is."

"I'm staying at the Princess. You could come to my room—"

"Too far. If I walk, I will be seen on the boulevard and picked up by the police or one of our guards." She glanced at the door again.

"Can you take a taxi? I can give you the fare."

"No, the drivers know the club whores. Unless I am with a john, I have no reason to go to a fancy hotel where security would stop me at the door. Besides, the drivers are rewarded for their information. Even if I could meet with you at the

Princess, someone from the club might pick me up on my way out."

I hated to think of this girl spending one more minute in this place, let alone the rest of the night with one man after another. I was positive now that she needed my help and I wanted to hug her for her bravery.

"What if I have a man escort you? Do you ever have clients take you back to their hotel?"

"Yes, but it is very expensive and it doesn't happen very often." Looking down at her hands twisting the hem of her shirt, she shook her head.

"If you need to walk out with a client, I'll get you one. Give me time to talk to the man at my table. He'll be your way out of the club."

"Really?" Her face lit up with surprise and hope. She glanced again at the door. "They will wonder what's taking me so long in the bathroom. I've got to go."

"First, tell me your name."

"Nadine ... Nadine Williams."

"I'm Deanne." Her thoughts broadcasted loud and clear. Taking such a big chance on me scared her to death. "Doing this took a lot of courage. I promise I'll do everything I can to help you."

She hurried out of the door.

I wanted to allow her a few minutes before I came out. As I waited, another young woman staggered into the ladies' room wearing a white lace mini-dress. I hoped she was not at the club alone then noticed a large rock of a wedding ring.

I left the restroom and headed back to our table. Sandy was

dancing with a handsome young man of her age with clean-cut hair and casual clothes. Most likely an American tourist, I thought. But I didn't sense any sort of threat from him. However, Faye Franklin and her girlfriends had thought the same way about Alex James-or-Jones, so I kept a close watch.

José was also on the dance floor, his attention on his pretty partner.

I had almost reached our booth when I sensed something drawing my attention to a darkened corner in the back of the room.

Sitting on a bar stool at a tall table, our bodyguard Pete was keeping us in his line of sight. Raising a drink to his mouth, he looked at me over the rim of the glass and then lowered it.

Without showing any sign of recognition, I continued to my table and slid in next to Alicia.

Keeping her voice low, she described watching the young woman follow me to the restroom. "After a few minutes, the security guy started looking for her. I was on my way to warn you when she came out. He stopped her and raised his fist like he would hit her. Instead, he tapped his wristwatch, chewing her out." Then Alicia chuckled.

I frowned. "What's so funny?"

"While he was in her face, he didn't notice her hand reaching into her purse until she held a tampon in front of his nose." Alicia laughed then pressed her lips tight. "You'd have thought it was a snake from the way his head jerked back. He just turned and walked away."

Men were predictable, no matter the culture. I grinned. "Way to go, Nadine."

"So, you did talk to her."

"Yes, and she needs our help. I didn't get any more information from her, but I have a plan."

Sandy returned to our booth, several steps ahead of José—each taking a different path through the maze of tables. They had to maintain the charade of being friends, not a couple. After I filled them in about Nadine Williams, I saw José's eyes narrow and his brow furrow.

"If I walk out of here with her, how will the three of you get back to the hotel? Doing that is not safe. You should have a man with you."

"We will," I said with a subtle jerk of my head. "Pete's here. You leave with Nadine, and he'll follow us."

Alicia asked, "How can we let him know about the change in plans?"

"Sandy will tell him."

"Me?" She leaned forward and whispered, "Why? How? I don't know where he is."

"I do."

Sandy, José and Alicia turned toward me with wide-eyed stares.

Then Alicia narrowed her gaze. "You spotted him just like you did in Mexico City. He must not be very good if you keep seeing him following us."

"He's very good," I said in his defense. "I seem to have a sixth sense with radar."

They assumed I was joking and they chuckled.

I gave Sandy instructions about Pete's location in the back of the room. "You'll send a drink to his table with a note to ask him to dance. Even if the waitress reads it, she won't think the request is unusual."

A short time later, Nadine abandoned the man at the bar and talked with a few other men before José approached her and asked her to dance. After a few songs, José guided Nadine to our booth.

He introduced everyone. "I hope you don't mind if the lady and I move to that empty table."

"Not at all," I answered, playing along. "We'll be perfectly fine."

Alicia added, "We'll get a taxi back to the hotel."

"Are you sure?" José acted uncertain.

Nadine pressed herself against him, slipping her arms around his waist.

"We're big girls," Sandy said a little too defensively. I sensed a hint of jealousy. "We can find our way home."

Nervous sweat beaded on his forehead.

Come on, José. You can do this.

He glanced at me as if he heard my plea. His demeanor changed as he squared his shoulders.

"Very well." He gave a slight nod to us as he slid his arm around Nadine's waist and pressed her to his side. "I will see you in the morning. *Buenas noches, señoras y señorita.*"

He escorted Nadine to the vacant booth where she slid to the back and waved at a passing waitress.

The girls obviously knew each other, which could aid our investigation. I wondered if the pretty waitresses were expected to serve more than drinks to the male patrons.

The female singer in the band spoke into her microphone,

"We are taking a little break after this next song. It's going to be a slow one. So, gentlemen, here's your chance to have a little romance with your lady."

José walked by our table and gave us a smile as he held Nadine's hand, leading her back to the dance floor.

Sandy avoided looking at them. Instead, she focused on her nearly empty wine glass, circling the rim with her index finger.

The music started and the singer began "Saving All My Love for You," another song by Whitney Houston.

Pete appeared at Sandy's side, holding up a slip of paper between his fingers. He looked at her, then glanced at Alicia and me before turning his attention back to her.

She practically leapt to her feet and allowed him to lead her to the dance floor.

I watched them as Alicia turned to me. "I have to tell you I'm a little worried about getting sidetracked with Nadine."

I acknowledged her concern with a nod but added a shrug. "You would have done the same thing if the shoe was on the other foot."

"You're right." She sighed. "But we have to be careful. What if she isn't really in trouble? What if we've aroused someone's suspicion and Nadine has been sent to expose us? We have to act like ordinary tourists who wouldn't have a clue what to do other than take her to the American consulate."

"We can't assume any government official, U.S. or Mexican, hasn't been paid off by the same people who handle Nadine."

"And those same people might have Faye."

I saw the realization in her gaze. "Just play along with me.

I'm not the type of person to wring my hands or pace the floor. But if that's what I need to do to appear like a nervous tourist in Nadine's eyes, I'll do it. Meanwhile, we'll pretend to stumble our way through figuring out how to help her get out of the country."

She opened her mouth and then clamped it shut, shaking her head in disbelief.

I rested my hand on Alicia's wrist. "I realize we know absolutely nothing about Nadine but I can't turn my back on her."

Sandy returned to our table, and I didn't need to ask how it went with Pete. I had already observed how his body language changed on the dance floor. He was not happy.

Alicia asked, "What did Pete have to say?"

"Aside from the fact that rescuing Nadine is an inconvenient interruption in our investigation," she began, pointedly staring at me, "he said she cannot be seen leaving with José, even if you are trying to make it look like she's landed a high-paying client."

I frowned. "We can't leave her here. I promised to help, and I don't go back on my promises."

Sandy held up her hand to stop me. "Pete already assumed you'd feel that way. He's got a different plan."

If I trusted Ricardo, I had to trust Pete, too. "I'm listening."

"First, he wants me to pretend I'm jealous of Nadine so I can get close enough to José to tell him that Pete's waiting to talk in the men's room. Then I throw a drink in his face so he has an excuse to go to the restroom."

I sensed Sandy could pull off the drama without much

effort. "Okay, so that's how Pete will explain the change in plans. But how does he propose to get Nadine out of the club tonight?"

"You had said Nadine is free to go out alone during the day, right?"

"Yes." I wasn't comfortable where the conversation was headed.

"José will tell Nadine to go to the nearby marketplace at ten tomorrow morning where Pete will meet up with her. He'll bring her into the hotel through the guest garage and take the rear elevator to our floor."

Alicia turned to me. "You have to admit that's a safer strategy for everyone involved."

After running through that plan again, I nodded. "I hope Nadine understands and goes along with it."

"They're coming back from the dance floor." Sandy turned her gaze to me, waiting for my go-ahead.

"Do it," I said.

José and Nadine approached their booth, and Sandy got up, taking her cocktail. He waited next to his table while Nadine sat and slid over to make room.

Sandy marched two steps toward him. "José!"

He spun to face her, confusion on his face. "Sandy? Wha—?"

Before she allowed him to finish, she was toe to toe with him. I have to give her credit for a convincing acting job. She may have been urging him to play along but she made it look like she was mad as hell.

With her drink glass in one hand, she raised her other hand, poking him in the chest.

He leaned back, bumping into the edge of the table. Patrons were beginning to notice.

Nadine glanced toward the bar and back at José. Her gaze met mine for a fleeting moment. She couldn't risk acknowledging me, but I knew she wanted to ask what was happening.

Sandy swayed as if she was having a hard time keeping her balance. "I have been practically throwing myself at you for days, and you want *her?* Whaz wrong? Why don't you want *me?*"

José reached out to steady her. "Sandy, please don't make a scene."

"I'll make a scene if I damn well wanna make a scene!" She took a big swig of her cocktail and spewed it on the front of his shirt.

Someone nearby whooped in delight. Others cheered her on in English and Spanish. She brought her hand back as if she was going to slap José.

He grabbed her wrist. "That's enough," he warned her.

"Oh, yeah?" She smirked, throwing the rest of her drink in his face.

José dropped her arm and jumped back, cursing a blue streak while wiping the alcohol from his eyes with the cuff of his shirt.

Nadine jumped up with a napkin to help him. He couldn't see who was there and shoved her away. "José, it's me."

He squinted at her. "Oh! I'm sorry, Nadine."

"Let's get you cleaned up," she offered as she linked her

hand through his elbow. "Let me help you to the restroom."

"No!" José and Sandy said in unison.

Lifting a hand in a stop motion, he added, "I can make it on my own. Wait here. I'll be back in few minutes."

Nadine watched him take a few steps before he bumped into a chair. She started toward him but Sandy blocked her path, getting in her face. Whatever Sandy said was under her breath. Nadine turned and returned to the booth she'd shared with José.

Sandy remained in the aisle, crossed her arms and stared at Nadine who crossed her own arms and leaned back, the image of stubborn defiance.

Alicia went over to Sandy, put her hand gently on her arm and coaxed her back to the table. Of course, her gesture was all for show.

Sandy slumped into her seat, her back to the booth where Nadine sat, muttering about the loss of her drink.

I leaned forward to speak to her without being overheard. "If that was an audition for undercover work, you passed with flying colors."

The corners of Sandy's mouth twitched, trying hard not to break into a smile.

"What did you say to Nadine?" Alicia asked.

"Play along, and José will explain later."

Soon, he rejoined Nadine who fawned over him, stroking his cheek and nuzzling his neck. Intentional or not, he kept glancing at the back of Sandy's head.

Finally, he turned to face Nadine, leaned close and spoke. She nodded solemnly, adding an effective little pout of disappointment. He got up to let her out of the booth. She rested her hand on his chest and walked her fingers up toward his neck, a last gesture of seduction, then gave him a light shove and walked away with the exaggerated hip-sway of a hooker. Male heads swiveled as she passed.

José plopped down hard on the bench, shoulders slumped.

I watched her circle the far side of the club, letting the men get a good look. Along the back wall of tall tables, a secluded group of four young men in the corner called her over. My gut twisted into a knot. They were very drunk. One of them stuffed folded bills into her cleavage, distracting her while two of his friends surrounded her. She tried to push them away but they were bigger and stronger. In the smoky darkness, they shoved her behind them toward the fourth friend while the three buddies blocked anyone from seeing what was happening behind them.

The band played a loud rock song that was sure to drown out any screams.

I couldn't sit there, knowing what was about to happen. "Nadine's in trouble," I said.

"We know but we can't do anything until tomorrow," Alicia's forearm rested on the table as she tapped the base of her glass.

"I mean right now." I forced the words through clenched teeth. "I've got to stop it."

"What? Where?" Alicia and Sandy sat upright and looked around, alerting José at the other booth.

"In the back corner." I started to head in that direction when I spotted Pete.

His gaze followed my gesture toward the suspicious lineup of three young men. Pete gave me a subtle wave of his hand to warn me back. He was closer and could investigate the situation faster than I could.

From what I could see, they weren't going to let him disrupt their fun. Heart pounding double time, I glanced around the club, looking for the guard at the bar. He was gone.

All I could think about was Pete taking on four men who were close to half his age.

As soon as the band finished their song, Nadine let out an angry scream. The three young men froze. Pete gut-punched one guy who doubled over, revealing the assault taking place behind him. Men at nearby tables jumped into action, launching a brawl.

José rushed up to me. "We need to get Nadine out of here. Now!"

I shook my head and rested a staying hand on his arm. "Pete won't let her get hurt."

"*We* need to get out of here. Now!" Alicia echoed, joining us. Sandy was by her side.

Pete emerged from the melee with Nadine under one arm, guiding her toward the bar.

Her long blonde hair was a mess, some of it hanging over her face. When she shoved it out of her eyes, she glared with anger.

Not the tears and devastation I'd thought I'd see. The girl surprised me with her grit.

Two of the club's girls rushed toward her.

In a flash, Pete said something to Nadine.

She looked up, her mouth slack-jawed.

He smiled, gripped her shoulders and steered her into the arms of her friends.

As they whisked her away, she twisted around to stare at the man who'd rescued her.

Now that I knew Nadine was safely out of harm's way, I was more than happy to get back to our hotel.

CHAPTER 11

August 25, 1990
Saturday, 10:35 a.m.

Sitting by the window of our hotel room with the morning sun illuminating her pale skin, Nadine looked so much younger without the smoky eyes and red lips she'd worn in the nightclub. Her long blonde hair was pulled up into a high ponytail. In the baby blue t-shirt and cut-off jeans, she could have been a typical American teenager hanging out at the mall.

Except for the fear in her eyes.

As planned, Pete had picked up Nadine at the marketplace and brought her to the hotel, taking the back elevator to our floor. Staying to listen to what she had to say, he leaned against the wall by the door. José stood next to him. Alicia and Sandy sat in the two remaining chairs while I chose the edge of my bed, my knees nearly touching Nadine's.

Her thin arms folded across her chest. With her hands cupping her elbows, she didn't try to hide the fresh bruises on her arms. Her right cheek and jaw were shadowed in purplish-blue and slightly swollen.

I sensed she had more injuries that were not visible. "I'm sorry about last night," I said. "If we had let you leave with José—"

She pointed at Pete. "He already explained on our way over here that this way was safer."

"Not entirely."

"It's not the first time I've been knocked around." She shifted and winced.

A sharp pain stabbed my chest. Flashes of her memory filled my mind like a choppy film reel. A fist to her ribs. Gasps for air. Face slammed to the table. Arms yanked behind her. The hem of her dress shoved to her waist. The searing pain in her vagina.

I hid my anguish over the brutality she'd endured. "Is there anything I can do?"

"No. I'll be okay." She glanced down. "What happened last night wasn't as bad as what will happen if they catch me trying to run away."

"Who are 'they'?" I made a mental note to jot this down when Nadine was out of sight.

"The people who keep us in line."

"Last night, you mentioned a farm. Can you tell me more about it?"

"I only know it's where they send girls who don't cooperate." Her fingers tightened around her elbows.

In my mind's eye, I received images similar to the previous night, except the sexual assaults came from her keepers, including the security man hanging around the bar.

Knowing about the terrible abuse Nadine had suffered at the club, I hated to think what it must be like for the girls at the farm. Was Faye one of those girls?

Her eyes narrowed as she glanced around the room at each

of us. "Who are you people?"

José snapped to attention. "I told you last night that I am their tour guide. They wanted to see the nightlife of Acapulco so I took them to the club."

She looked at Pete. "What about you? What's your story? Why weren't you sitting with them last night at the club?"

"That's strictly a need-to-know basis." He narrowed his gaze and jerked his chin up. "And you don't need to know."

She frowned and studied me again. "Why are you so willing to help me? I don't get it."

"I have a daughter, Nadine. If she were in your place, I hope someone would do the same thing for her." Remembering to act as if I was a naïve tourist, I added, "We should call the U.S. Consulate."

She hit her legs with her fists. "No!"

"Why not?" I kept up the pretense. "They would help you."

She shook her head. "You don't understand. Tourists don't know what it's really like. The bribes. The pay-offs. The snitch money. Maybe not everyone is dirty. But only one call is enough to get me in trouble."

"Then what do you want me to do? You're in trouble. And I want to help." I held my hands out. "I'm just not sure how."

She covered her face as she dissolved into sobs.

I wrapped my arms around her to console her. My heart sank as I picked up on her thoughts. She was pregnant. Not for the first time. And she was terrified she'd lose this one.

"I am in bigger trouble than you know." Her words were barely a whisper. She pulled back but refused to look up into my eyes. "I'm pregnant."

I heard José groan. *"¡Madre de Dios!"*

"When I saw them at your table—" She nodded at Alicia and Sandy. "—I started thinking if nobody looks twice at a mother and daughter having a nice time, maybe they wouldn't look twice at me being with you."

The room fell silent. I wasn't about to correct her mistaken assumption that Alicia and Sandy were mother and daughter, and I hoped they didn't, either.

She sighed heavily. "I know, it sounds crazy now. But the idea seemed like such a good one at the time. When I saw you walk by me on your way to the bathroom, I just knew if I didn't talk to you I'd miss the only chance of getting out of here."

I rested my hands on her shoulders and waited for her to look up. The sad desperation in her eyes made my heart ache. She was only one out of hundreds, probably thousands, of girls forced into the sex trade. "I don't think your idea is crazy, at all," I said. "In fact, it just might work."

Her misperception of the mother-daughter scenario started the wheels turning in my head. I didn't know how we would pull it off, but I would make sure Nadine was safely on a plane before I left Acapulco.

"Do you have a passport?" Pete asked.

Nadine slumped in the chair and shook her head. "It's gone."

"Then you need a copy of your birth certificate," Alicia said. "Your parents could—?"

"No." She sniffled.

I reached out and placed my hand on her knee. "Maybe it's

time you filled us in about yourself. Let's start with where you're from."

"Alabama," she said. "First Montgomery. Then Birmingham. My father died when I was little. Momma died four years ago. Since then, I've been on my own."

Sandy asked, "How old were you?"

"Old enough to take care of myself."

As a minor, she should have entered the foster system. Sitting in front of us without makeup, she looked about sixteen.

"How *did* you take care of yourself?" Sandy's voice was quiet and gentle as if talking to a child, which wasn't too far from the truth.

Nadine's posture relaxed. "Momma had been sick in bed for a while so I learned how to sign the Social Security checks we'd been getting since my daddy died. After her passing, I kept cashing the checks and paying our rent, telling the property manager she was still in bed. But I came home one day and found him waiting in the apartment. I told him I'd taken her to the hospital in the middle of the night but he didn't believe me. He said he was calling people to come get me. So I took off."

She paused, lost in the past. We sat in silence for a few moments until she was able to continue.

She leaned forward on her elbows and clasped her hands together. "I dropped out of school and got a cheap room in a sleazy hotel on the west side. I tried to find a job but there wasn't anything so I left town. Ended up in New Orleans."

I thought to myself how Nadine had been the perfect target

for the men who lure naïve young girls into the sex trade.

She intertwined her fingers. "I was hanging around by Café du Monde one afternoon when a really cute guy told me I looked like a supermodel. He was a photographer and offered to help me start a modeling career." She shook her head. "I thought Marvin would be my ticket out of my dead-end life, and I was willing to sleep with him to get it. Not like I was saving myself for marriage, thanks to my uncle."

Sandy gasped. "Your uncle?"

Nadine nodded. "About six months before Mamma got sick, he started coming over while she was at work, telling me he had to look out for me. I was so pretty he worried boys might take advantage of me. Since I didn't have a daddy to teach me about boys, he said he would. I was curious so I went along with him unzipping his pants and showing his cock. That's all, at first. He was so ... I don't know, sweet? I wanted to believe him! I told you I was stupid, didn't I?"

"No, not stupid. He was counting on your trust." My stomach tightened. My hunch was she had never told the full story about her uncle until now. The dam had burst. Details spilled from her like a flood of muddy water.

"Yeah-well ... he got me right where he wanted me. One minute he was fondling me and the next he was fucking me, saying he was sorry. Sorry! When he finished, he begged me to forgive him and not to tell Mamma. He said she'd kill both of us if she found out what we'd been doing for weeks. I was scared he might be right. He promised it wouldn't happen again so I agreed to keep my mouth shut. But he came over days later, crying and feeling so guilty about hurting me that he wanted to die. I was devastated that he would kill himself because of me."

Nadine stared at the floor and smiled a sad smile. "I panicked, thinking he would leave a tell-all suicide note about me seducing him. So I did the one thing that, I thought, would save his life and keep our secret safe. I took him to my bedroom. Every time my mamma was out of the apartment, he would knock on the door as if he had been waiting and watching for her to leave. One afternoon she came home early for a doctor's appointment and caught him in the act. The next day she and I moved to Birmingham and never spoke to anyone in her family again."

José clenched his fists and excused himself from the room.

Pete followed, although I doubt it was because he was shocked or upset, considering his years as a police officer.

Alicia and I exchanged a look of mild surprise. With our backs to the door, we'd both been too immersed in Nadine's story to remember the men were present, let alone that José was a school teacher, not an investigator. At least Sandy had gained something positive from her own brutal experience. For one so young, she had the stomach to deal with the underbelly of life.

After the interruption of the men's sudden departure, I wasn't sure if Nadine would continue. But she did.

"Marvin told me he could help me launch my modeling career if I went to the Mexican Riviera where the resorts use American models in their brochures. He said I could work at a club in Acapulco until he put together a portfolio. He'd even help me get my passport and buy my plane ticket. I didn't know he was bringing me down here to be a hooker. Once I was here, I didn't have any money to get home unless I turned tricks so I did what I had to do. At first, I got paid regularly so I stashed it in my room, hoping to save enough to go home."

I hated to push her for more details, but I hoped we might find out more information to help us in our search for Faye Franklin. "Did you see Marvin again?"

Again, she shook her head, picking at the hem of her skirt. "I got pregnant a few weeks later and told Geraldo—that's the manager—hoping he'd let me go home. But he got mad, saying I had to get an abortion because nobody will pay for a whore with a big, ugly belly. And if I didn't get the abortion, I'd have to watch him sell the baby to cover the money lost while I was too fat to work. I asked for Marvin. But Geraldo said he didn't know anybody by that name."

Alicia asked, "Didn't you have the money to leave by then? You said you were being paid."

"Not enough for airfare, but I thought I could take a bus if I could get my passport."

"But they took it," I said, knowing all too well how this sleazy industry worked.

"Yeah. Geraldo originally said he'd keep it safe for me in his office. I asked for it, but he acted like he didn't know anything about it. I got so mad that he locked me in my room. A while later, he sent a doctor to examine me, to find out if I was really pregnant and to get rid of my baby. I wasn't even allowed to go to a clinic. The guard was outside the door with a bucket, towels and a plastic sheet."

Sandy sucked in a breath, and then realized her shocked

response had drawn our attention.

She gave me an apologetic look but I couldn't be upset with her. I had a feeling we would hear a lot worse. The more I heard from Nadine, the more I feared for Faye Franklin.

Looking down, Nadine gently slid one hand over her belly. "I got really sick with an infection afterward. I thought I couldn't get pregnant again. But just in case I did, I saved and saved until I had a couple thousand dollars stashed under my mattress. And then one day, the money was gone."

"Gone?" Sandy asked, leaning forward. "Stolen?"

Nadine nodded.

"Of course, without a passport you couldn't even open a bank account" Alicia said.

"The other girls said the banks weren't safe. When I tore my room apart looking for the money, I found a hidden camera. I ran out, screaming and cussing and swearing I was going to kill Geraldo. The guards tackled me just as I got to his office and put me in lock-down."

"Lock-down?" Sandy asked, leaning forward.

"A tiny little room with no windows and just a dim light bulb hanging from the ceiling. There's just a filthy old cot, a nasty-looking toilet and a security camera high on the wall. My food and water were shoved through a slot in the door."

"How long were you there?" Sandy's voice was hushed and horrified.

"I lost track of time. I only found out later I was in there a couple weeks. They'd given me water to drink that had tasted strange but I got so thirsty I didn't care. Things got fuzzy. I figured they'd slipped me some drugs. I was never sure if I was awake or dreaming." Nadine shuddered.

I almost did the same. I smelled mildew and stale sweat. I felt bugs crawling on my skin. I heard skittering of rodents.

"Eventually, Geraldo asked if I was ready to behave myself, and I said yes. I got outside, and the sunlight was so bright that it hurt my eyes." With a grimace of pain, she shut her eyes tight, pinching the bridge of her nose.

I felt my own energy drop and I knew I was sensing her exhaustion. I checked my watch and saw the time was quarter to noon. "Sandy, would you mind staying with Nadine while Alicia and I go next door to talk to José?"

"Not at all."

Nadine yawned. "Trust me. I'm not going anywhere. If you want to go with them, I'll be fine by myself." A knock on the door startled her. She sat up straight, her eyes open wide in panic.

"Yo estoy aquí para limpiar su habitación." I am here to clean your room.

I patted Nadine's knee. "Only the maid."

Alicia cracked open the door to answer. *"No hay limpieza. Muchas gracias."*

A soft voice on the other side asked if she should come back later. Alicia told her it would not be necessary for today, thanked her again and started to close the door.

I called out for her to wait while I took some *pesos* from my purse.

The maid initially refused.

I'm sure it seemed like a large amount of money for essentially doing nothing. But the coins were equivalent to only a few American dollars.

After the door clicked shut, I turned back to Nadine. "Try to relax. No one knows you're here. Why don't you lie down on my bed and rest for a few minutes?"

She nodded mutely but didn't move.

Knowing how tired she must be, I walked over to her and cupped my hand under her elbow to coax her up. With a heavy sigh, she allowed me to guide her. She curled up on her side, and I covered her with a spare blanket from the closet.

Her fingers closed over mine. She gave me a tired smile. "Thank you."

"You're welcome. We'll be back soon." I looked at Sandy and jerked my head toward the next room. "Holler if you need us."

CHAPTER 12

August 25, 1990
Saturday, 12:10 p.m.

Alicia and I left and walked next door to José's room. After we were inside, Alicia produced the tape recorder hidden in her pocket and played the recording of our talk with Nadine.

José turned away and looked out the window. "This isn't what I expected when Ricardo hired me. I was excited to be a part of this investigation. But I don't know if I have the stomach for it."

"José, you are a good person with a great deal of compassion. It's that same compassion that makes us do what we do. If we didn't care so much, we wouldn't be here."

"We can't save all of them, Deanne."

"I know." I sighed and shook my head. "One at a time, José. That's better than none at all."

He glanced over his shoulder at Alicia, then at me. "Ricardo should be told about all of this."

"That's why I made an excuse to check with you," I said. "I couldn't call him while Nadine was in the room and my portable phone isn't getting reception."

He gestured at the phone on the night stand. "It is all yours."

I doubted Ricardo would be in his office on a Saturday, but I tried the number anyway. No luck. In case of emergency, he'd given us the number of his cellular phone.

After listening to six rings, I was about to hang up when he answered, "Perez."

"Hello, Ricardo. It's Deanne Acuña." I assured him all of us were fine. Then I sprung the news about our night at the club. "I know the Franklins expect us to be looking for their daughter, and we are. I believe Nadine has given us valuable information about a farm where we could find Faye. But I simply can't leave without getting Nadine out."

He was silent for a long moment. "She said she has no passport, yes?"

"Right."

"No problemo."

"I was hoping you would say that. How long will it take?"

"Only a matter of hours—"

"Great!"

"—*after* I get her photo."

"I'll take a picture. But how do I get it to you?"

"Let me know when you think it will be ready, and I'll send someone on the next flight to Acapulco. I can arrange her flight to the U.S. at the same time. Where will she be going?"

"Los Angeles, hopefully. I have a friend who owns several apartment buildings, and I'll ask if she has any vacancies. I'll call you later today."

After I hung up, I heard José breathe a sigh of relief.

"Sounds like Ricardo reacted better than I thought he would."

I grinned. "A little advice, José— It's always better to imagine the best-case scenario than worry about the worst."

He flashed a grin. "I will keep that in mind."

Alicia spoke. "You mentioned getting a photo of Nadine."

"Yes. In disguise, though. Ricardo is sending someone over from his office to pick it up as soon as we can have one ready. We should get the passport by tomorrow morning."

José appeared surprised. "I really don't see how we can keep pretending we're just tourists, especially when we will be getting her a new passport and disguising her appearance."

I agreed. "She's suspicious about our motives, and I can't say I blame her, considering what she's been through."

Alicia frowned, worry written on her face. "Do you think Nadine would tell someone if she knew our real reason for being here? What if she goes back to the owner of the club?"

"She won't," I said, unable to express to them how I knew. "I'm sure she's telling the truth."

"How can you be positive?" José asked.

"I trust my gut." I waited for their rebuttal but heard none. "Nadine deserves our honesty, but we can be selective in what we tell her. We certainly won't supply names or details."

Alicia added, "She already thinks I'm Sandy's mother."

"Yes, I know. Let's stick with that. We'll also keep up the pretense of being shop owners on a buying trip. But we'll tell her that I am searching for a twenty-two-year-old niece with drug problems and a record of prostitution."

"As an adult, this fictitious niece can't be forced to return to the states," Alicia said, clearly knowing the ins and outs of the law. "So, what excuse do we have for looking for her?"

"I'll say that my brother and his wife want to know if she's still alive. The responsibility will be theirs to come and get her."

"Do you think Nadine will buy such a story?" José asked.

"It will go a long way to explain why we are not acting like your average, everyday tourist, and why we're willing to get her out of the country." I felt my stomach growl and covered it with my hand.

Alicia smiled and gestured toward it. "Time for lunch?"

"You two can head downstairs to get something to eat while I make one more phone call. When I'm done here, I'll send Sandy to join you."

"What about you and Nadine?" José asked.

"I'll order room service. We don't want to risk someone seeing Nadine in the coffee shop."

"Exactly," Alicia said, "And after we eat, we'll get my supplies from the van to experiment with disguises on Nadine this afternoon. So, don't start to worry if we're gone a little longer."

"Thanks for letting me know."

After they left, I dialed the Massachusetts number of my former client Lisa Norris, now known as Elizabeth Diamond. I had been referred to her because of my experience with helping abused women relocate with new identities. Lisa was on the run, hiding from her oldest brother who had killed their parents and left their younger brother for dead. After learning of his arrest and subsequent escape, I became involved in the long manhunt spanning five states. In the end, he went to prison while Lisa and her kid brother inherited millions in real estate and started a new life on the East Coast. But we still kept in touch.

I heard Lisa's voice on her answering machine, but the call was dropped before I could leave a message. I tried again.

She picked up on the second ring, sounding a little out of breath. She recognized my voice immediately. "I was just coming in the door when I heard the phone ringing a minute ago but I didn't catch it in time. Was that you?"

"Yes. I'm calling from Acapulco and I was cut off."

"As much as I'm happy to hear from you, I'm guessing this isn't a social call."

"Unfortunately, no. I have a problem, and I hope you can help me." I relayed the story in as few words as possible.

"What? Wait a minute. I thought you went to Mexico to look for a girl named Faye, not Nadine."

"I still am. This is just a little diversion."

"Little? Hardly." She chuckled, and her voice softened. "Oh, Deanne, you have such a huge heart. If not for you, I don't know what I would've done. I told you I wanted to help if you ever needed anything. What can I do?"

"Nadine needs a place to live. Could she stay in one of your apartment buildings in L.A.?" Most of the Diamond Enterprises properties were in Southern California. I knew of some in Hawaii but paradise was too expensive for a young woman trying to make a new life for herself and a baby.

"I'll call my property manager to find out if any of the furnished apartments are available."

"Even if it's empty, Kitty could buy things from a thrift store for Nadine to get by."

"Kitty *is* resourceful," Lisa said

I noted the admiration in her tone. During the months we hid Lisa at our house, she and my eighteen-year-old daughter had become such good friends that Kitty now worked part-time as an assistant for Lisa. Long-distance, of course. Primarily, Kitty forwarded mail from a post office box Lisa kept for security reasons.

"I'll call Stephen right away," Lisa said. "Do you want him to call Kitty?"

"Let me get a hold of her first. She would have no idea what he was talking about. Why don't you let me give his number to her?"

"Hold on while I get my DayRunner." Lisa came back on the line and read her property manager's number. "Do you have money for her airfare? I'd be more than happy to wire some to you."

"We have that covered but thank you for the offer."

"What about when she gets to L.A.? If you think she's capable of basic office skills, I could find her a job with one of our companies."

My heart warmed with the generosity of this young woman. "I have a feeling she could handle just about anything."

Lisa chuckled again. "I've learned never to doubt those gut instincts of yours."

I smiled to myself. Lisa had been fascinated by my intuition, asking me all sorts of questions while she stayed with me. She was well aware my clairvoyance had contributed to the apprehension of her brother in New Mexico.

After saying goodbye, I hung up the phone, relieved

Nadine had somewhere to go. I made a quick call to Kitty who had already sensed something was brewing. She was eager to help. I thanked her and told her I'd get back to her when I had more information.

My hand lingered on the cradled receiver as Ryan popped into my head. I considered calling him while I had the chance. We hadn't talked in nearly a week, and I didn't know when I'd have another opportunity for a private conversation.

Promising myself that I would keep it short, I picked up the receiver again. At the end of the fourth ring, the answering machine played a greeting by Ryan. I was disappointed but not surprised. After all, today was Saturday. He could have his sons visiting for the weekend.

After the standard beep, I started to leave a message.

But his voice interrupted me. "Hello? Deanne? Is that you?" He sounded sleepy.

"Yes, it's me. Did I wake you?"

"Believe it or not, I actually fell asleep in the hammock in the backyard." His voice cracked, and he cleared his throat.

"I only have a couple minutes."

"If a couple minutes is all I get, I'll take it. How are you? How's the investigation going?"

I gave him the fastest rundown I could manage.

He listened, then said. "I miss you."

My heart ached. "I miss you, too."

"About this girl you're helping ..."

"Yes?"

"You're putting yourself in danger."

"Maybe. Probably. But Nadine is in even greater danger if

we don't get her out."

"Be careful."

"I will. I have to go, Ryan. I don't know when I'll be able to call again."

"Stay safe. I love you."

I swallowed hard over the lump in my throat. "I love you, too."

CHAPTER 13

August 25, 1990
Saturday, 12:45 p.m.

I returned to my room and spotted Sandy sitting cross-legged on the floor, twisting her torso in a familiar yoga pose. She looked at me and raised her finger to her lips. Nadine was asleep.

Keeping my voice to a whisper, I suggested she join José and Alicia in the restaurant for lunch. She nodded and quietly slipped out.

Only a few short minutes later, Nadine woke with a gasp. After a quick look around, she realized immediately she was not in any danger. Taking a deep breath, she rested her forearm over her eyes.

I didn't need her to explain the sudden nightmare. Her terror had telepathically relayed images of an enormous shadowy monster chasing her down a dark alley.

She lifted her arm enough to spot me. "I sure wish I could shut my eyes just once without scaring myself awake."

I smiled.

"What's so funny?"

"Nothing, really. I haven't heard you talk with such a thick Southern accent."

"Yeah-well, every once in a while it just comes out when I'm too tired to stop it."

"Why would you stop it?"

"When I first got here, I was so embarrassed when everyone made fun of me, especially when some of those old Southern sayings didn't make sense to anybody else but me. Instead of my name, I was called *la puta estúpida*. So I tried real hard to lose my accent."

I was sorry my smile had reminded her of the torment directed her way. I suspected others were jealous or felt threatened by the new girl in the club, and the easiest target was her Southern accent and mannerisms. "I think your accent is very lovely. I hope you won't feel you have to hide it when you are living in Los Angeles."

"What?" She scrambled on all fours to the edge of the bed. "I'm going to L.A.?"

I grinned at her burst of energy and enthusiasm. "A friend of mine will let you stay in one of her apartments while you get on your feet."

"Did you tell her I was pregnant?"

"Yes. And that you needed a job."

Nadine slumped and crossed her arms. "Doing what? I don't know how to do anything."

"I told her you are smart and very capable of learning office skills. Most importantly, you need a job with medical benefits."

She narrowed her gaze, her lips pressed into a thin line. I couldn't blame her for being wary of my motives, considering all of the people who had used and abused her.

"I want to know what you get for helping me."

"A good feeling."

"What else?"

"Nothing more." I shook my head and smiled.

Her mind was swirling with conflicting emotions. She had risked everything to approach me, a perfect stranger. Now that she was with me, she couldn't quite let go of the fear and doubts. She wanted to trust me. No, not just wanted. She *had* to trust me ... and that scared her to death. I seemed nice enough. All of us seemed nice enough. She suspected we were too good to be true. She had never caught a break. Now that she had one, she found the fact too difficult to believe.

Without saying a word, she reached into one side of her bra and brought out some sort of jewelry in her clenched hand. I could see a bit of gold and a flash of sparkle. Then she pulled something out of the other side of her bra.

She extended her hands and opened her fingers. In her palms lay a tangle of gold chains, bracelets and rings, some adorned with diamonds.

"If you can sell them, you could buy my plane ticket and get a few hundred dollars for me until I find work."

During my investigations of designer knock-offs, I had acquired some abilities to differentiate between costume jewelry and the real deal, which these seemed to be. "If you don't mind my asking, where did you get them?"

"Sometimes my regulars give me presents." She paused, watching me. "You think I stole them, don't you?"

"I'm only wondering how you managed to keep them after your money was taken from your room."

"I ... um, found a better hiding place."

I really didn't want, or need, more details. "Put away your jewelry. Your plane ticket is already covered."

She hesitated before she slowly closed her hands. "I'll pay you back some day."

"That isn't necessary. Someday, you'll have an opportunity to help someone else."

"Not like this," she answered, stuffing the jewelry back in her bra. "I'll never forget what y'all are doing for me."

I smiled again.

"Uh-oh." Her face suddenly went pale. She clapped her hand over her mouth and dashed for the bathroom, leaving the door open behind her.

I doubted she was throwing up from the flu.

She emerged a few minutes later, looking wrung out and apologetic. "I'm either throwing up at all hours of the day, or I'm falling asleep at the drop of a hat."

"I suppose now isn't a good time to ask if you want me to order lunch."

"I only get nauseous just before I puke. Afterwards, I could eat a horse."

"How about hamburger?"

"Perfect."

"While we're waiting, why don't you enjoy a nice long soak in the tub?"

She perked up. "Mmmmm, that sounds like heaven."

«—»

After our lunch was delivered, Nadine came out of the bathroom wearing a white bathrobe with the logo of the

Princess Hotel. Her hair was wrapped in a towel. We sat at the small table to eat, and I quickly confessed about the search for my niece.

"Be careful about snooping around for information," she said.

I lifted the cover off my broiled fish. "That's why I didn't tell you the reason we were at the club last night. We didn't know if we could trust you."

"Now I understand why you've been asking so many questions." She opened a packet of catsup and squeezed it on her French fries. "Do you have a picture of your niece? Maybe I've seen her."

A photo? I hadn't thought far enough ahead to realize Nadine might offer to help. I had to come up with a good excuse.

I shook my head. "We need to look like we're only here to shop for our store. If our van is searched for any reason, we don't want the police to find a bunch of pictures. As you know, not all of the officers can be trusted."

She nodded. "Yeah. If any of them recognized her picture, they'd make up some reason to take you in for questioning. Who knows how long they'd keep you."

"Exactly." I cut a piece of my fish and speared it with my fork. "I have been meaning to ask if you know where the farm is located."

"In a jungle somewhere in Central America."

"Do you know what country?"

She shook her head and took another bite of burger, answering with her mouth full. "Nobody who was sent there ever came back."

"How many were sent?" My senses were pulling at me with some urgency. I *knew* this place held meaning. I just wasn't sure the meaning had to do with Faye.

"Um, three or four that I know of."

"How did you find out about them?"

"We all talk."

"The girls?"

"The girls and the guards."

"Did you ever talk to the owner of the club?"

"Never. And there's more than one owner. I don't know exactly how many or who they are. Important-looking men come in the club all the time. Maybe they were owners. Maybe only one was an owner, and the rest were his friends or owners of other clubs." She shrugged. "I don't know."

"What did they look like? Was there anything about any of them that stood out? The way they dressed. Color of their skin? Any scars?"

"Most looked pretty much the same in their suits. Some were darker brown than others. Some were lighter. I suppose they were Mexican but they could've been from Guatemala or El Salvador. Hell, they could've been Columbian, for all I know."

I switched the conversation back to the girls, hoping to gain more insight into Faye's situation.

"You were brought here with a promise of a good job until your modeling career took off. Were the others tricked, too?"

"Not all of them. Some were street hookers and saw the clubs as a move up the food chain. Some need the money for their drugs. A lot were poor like me and don't have anywhere else to go. After my lock-down, Geraldo said he was putting my money into a retirement account for when I got too old to work at the club. But he was lying. One of the guards told me I'd never leave. I was their property.

I continued eating my lunch, allowing her to talk freely and making our conversation less like an interrogation.

"I heard from the girls someone else had stashed her money in her room and got robbed, too. She was sent to another club before I got here. As far as I know, everybody else keeps their money in the office."

"They didn't have any problem getting it whenever they wanted?"

"Nope. Geraldo knows which ones are junkies so he gives them money to buy drugs. As long as they can work to get high they won't leave. The rest of us get just enough to buy underwear or go to a beauty salon. I never heard anyone complain or try to get back all their money." She paused. "Do you think any of this will help you find your niece?"

"That's what I'm hoping."

A few minutes later, I carried our lunch trays into the hallway to leave for the staff to pick up. I saw Alicia, Sandy and José emerge from the elevator.

Alicia carried a brown paper bag.

"I thought you were bringing your other suitcase from the van."

"I only brought what I needed." She held up the bag in her hand. "I didn't want Nadine to ask questions about all of the other makeup, wigs and disguises."

"Good point," I said.

Reaching for the door knob to let us into the room, I realized the door had locked behind me.

Alicia held up her room key. "Allow me."

We walked into an empty room. José closed the door.

"Nadine?" I said. "You can come out now."

She popped her head up on the other side of the bed. "I waited but you didn't come back in right away. I thought something was wrong, so I hid."

"I'm sorry. I didn't mean to scare you. We have a friend who can get you a passport but we need a photo—preferably in disguise, as you'd be when you board the plane."

Alicia dropped her purse on the bed, pulled a small box from the paper sack in her arms and held it up for Nadine to see. "Medium chestnut brown. I hope you'll like the shade."

"I'd be happy with anything," she answered, hugging herself and looking hopeful.

I turned to Sandy and José. "You two are elected to go shopping. Nadine will need two or three outfits that are plain and simple. We don't want anything that will draw attention to her. She'll also need pajamas, underwear and a small suitcase. Pick up basic toiletries, too. If her bag is inspected, it should contain the normal things a tourist would pack. Use your credit card, and I will reimburse you."

Sandy nodded, picked up a hotel note pad and pen, then looked at Nadine. "What's your size?"

"Six."

Sandy wrote the number. "And shoes?"

"Seven."

"Got it. We'll be back in a couple hours."

José held up his hand before I could speak. "I'll make sure Pete follows us."

After they left, Alicia started to work on Nadine. If I hadn't been there myself, I don't know if I would have recognized her with the short brown hair and the darkened skin from a tanning spray. Theatrical putty gave her a fuller jawline and altered her nose so it looked a little wider and a bit crooked, as if it had been broken.

When Sandy and José returned with several shopping bags and the suitcase, they stood slack-jawed at the transformation.

Sandy dropped everything and rushed up to Nadine, studying her from every angle. "Incredible. Even close up, it all looks so real."

"Thanks." Alicia folded her arms across her chest, beaming with pride.

"Now all we need is a photo for the passport," I said.

Nadine stared in awe into the mirror, her eyes liquid with emotion. "I can't believe this is actually happening," she whispered.

I nearly succumbed to tears myself.

CHAPTER 14

August 26, 1990
Sunday, 9:30 a.m.

After handing off Nadine's photo to Ricardo's courier, we stayed up late into the night, learning as much information about the clubs as possible. Ricardo confirmed the background information on Nadine and called in a favor to expedite the passport, which was expected to be ready by late afternoon. His courier would bring it to our hotel room, along with the plane ticket to Los Angeles.

However, all flights to Los Angeles were booked solid, including the Red Eye. No surprise there. After all, this week was the end of summer vacation for tourist families and college kids.

Our plans to visit the markets during the day and a club in the evening were put on hold one more day while we stayed with Nadine. José and Sandy were eager to continue searching Acapulco, but I didn't think we would find Faye here. From the moment I heard about the farm in Central America, I had a strong feeling we should head south.

José picked up some candy bars in the hotel gift shop along with a few magazines stocked for the American tourists and dumped them on the table in my hotel room. Sandy quickly snatched up *People* with Patrick Swayze on the cover. *Time* and *U.S. News & World Report* focused on troubles with Iraq. Alicia flipped through one of them while Nadine watched *Plaza Sésamo* on the television.

Sandy looked up. "You're watching Sesame Street?"

Nadine turned red. "I know it seems dumb, but I got hooked on it when I came here and didn't speak any Spanish. *Plaza Sésamo* reminded me of a happier time when I was a kid and my mom was still alive. The other girls teased me, but I learned Spanish by watching the show."

"That's cool," Sandy said.

"And smart," I added.

Staring at the TV, she didn't respond but the skeptical expression on her face told me that she didn't think of herself as smart. A survivor, maybe. But not smart.

I sat in front of her on the bed, blocking her view of the children's program. "Listen to me, Nadine. Having only an eighth grade education doesn't mean you're not intelligent. You had to drop out to take care of yourself."

"Yeah? Look how that turned out." She didn't meet my gaze. Instead, she bowed her head.

"You were only fourteen," I reminded her.

"So? I should've known better than to trust Marvin."

"Under a different set of circumstances, I might have agreed. But your mom just died. You didn't even have a chance to grieve before you were forced to live on the street. You were alone. And, I'll say it again, you were only fourteen."

Her hand slid over her belly. "I wouldn't be so scared if it was just me starting out all over again. But how can I take care of both of us when I don't even have a high school diploma?"

"You can study for a GED at night." I knew from her puzzled look that she had no idea what I meant. "Anyone who didn't graduate from high school can pass a series of tests to get a General Education Development credential. It's equivalent to a diploma and accepted for college entrance requirement."

"College?" She pushed herself upright. "Me?"

"Of course! If you want it, go for it."

A corner of her mouth tilted up in a hint of a smile. "Twenty-four hours ago, I wasn't sure if I was getting out of here. I can't believe I'm talking about going to college someday."

"Just remember you are smart enough to do anything you put your mind to. Promise?"

"I promise," she pledged, crossing her heart and then raising her hand.

"Good. Now I need to phone my daughter to check on the arrangements for your apartment." I rose and walked to the far side of Alicia's bed where the phone sat on the night stand.

Kitty answered right away.

As usual, our telepathic connection had already alerted her to my call.

"Hi, Mom. Lisa's manager gave me the address of an apartment complex in Hawthorne. It's not furnished, though. I found a few thrift stores that are open on Sunday. We'll head over this afternoon, then we'll buy some groceries."

"I knew you'd have it all under control."

"We're using Michael's van. Ryan also offered to help."

"He offered? Or did you ask him?"

She chuckled. "What do you think? He's not psychic. Of course, I asked him. He's family now, isn't he?"

"Well ..."

"'Nuff said."

I pictured her grinning like a Cheshire cat. She knew how Ryan and I felt about each other. My kids were happy for me and really liked Ryan.

"I didn't think to ask Nadine if there's anything she'd like from the store. Why don't I put her on so you can ask her and make a list?"

"Sure."

I motioned Nadine to the phone. "Kitty will be stocking your kitchen and needs to know what you like."

She scooted across the bed and tentatively took the receiver from my hand. "Hi, Kitty. This is Nadine."

After hearing Kitty explain the plans, Nadine answered, "I'm not picky about what I eat. I'm sure anything you get will be fine ... But, since you asked, I love Pop Tarts and Cap'n Crunch cereal. I really don't know how to cook anything, so I suppose some TV dinners would be good, especially anything with fried chicken."

Kitty said something that made Nadine smile wide and turn toward me. "She says you make the best fried chicken ever."

"I do! When I get home, I'll make it for you."

"Awesome! I'd like that." She went back to the phone. After a few more requests, she asked Kitty, "How will I find you when I land? What do you look like? What will you be wearing?"

She listened, nodding even though Kitty couldn't see her. "Okay. Got it. Thanks!"

When I accepted the receiver back from her, I instructed my daughter to contact Nick Oates, a homicide detective and long-time friend of mine. Nick was married to my college roommate, Christine. We had worked closely on my case involving the murder of Lisa's parents.

"Ask Nick to go with you to the airport when you pick up Nadine. She will have a new passport to go through customs but the photo will show her in disguise. If there is any problem with her appearance, she'll only have copies of her legal documents which might confuse matters. If that happens, Nick should be able to take care of the situation."

"Okay, I'll call him. And I still need her flight information. Do you have it?"

"She'll be on Mexicana Airlines coming in at the international terminal tomorrow afternoon." Ricardo had supplied the flight number and arrival time, which I passed along to Kitty. After a few more minutes of chit-chat about friends and neighbors back home, including my shepherd, Heidi, I thanked my daughter for all of her help. "I'll see you in a couple of weeks."

I hung up and looked at Nadine. "Don't worry. Everything will work out fine."

"Who is Nick Oates?"

"He's a very dear friend and a police detective."

"Police?" Panic filled her eyes.

Why was she scared? "Is there something I should know?"

"Um...no." She twisted a toe in the carpet.

"Nadine?"

"What if I'm not exactly eighteen yet? Will he turn me over to social services?"

"When is your birthday?" My muscles tensed as I wondered if I had yet another hurdle to deal with before we could continue our hunt for Faye.

"Next Sunday. September second."

I relaxed. "I'm willing to bet no one will want to go through the trouble of processing you as a minor. You'll be an adult before any paperwork would make it through the system."

"I hope you're right."

CHAPTER 15

August 27, 1990
Monday, 7:45 a.m.

The passport and airline ticket were delivered by the same courier twenty minutes earlier. Again, José, Sandy and Alicia had breakfast downstairs, and I stayed in the room with Nadine. The more time that passed since leaving the club, the more nervous she became.

I scanned the room service menu. "I'm ordering an omelet. What do you want?"

"Nothing for me. I'm not hungry."

A queasy feeling rose from my gut. I knew immediately that I was picking up on Nadine's symptoms of anxiety. "You should try to eat something. Maybe something light. You have a long day ahead."

"My stomach's got knots in it."

"You're nervous, which is understandable. But the longer you go on an empty stomach, the more likely you will get nauseous and light-headed. Your body needs nourishment for you and your baby now."

She sighed. "Okay. Then how about plain toast with jelly?"

"How about some protein?"

Grimacing, she shook her head. "Right now, just thinking

of eggs makes me want to barf."

"Well, you can have anything from the menu. The food doesn't have to be breakfast. What sounds good to you?"

"A banana sandwich on white bread with mayonnaise."

"I know about pregnancy cravings, but that's a new one on me."

"Not in Alabama. My momma used to make them for me. 'Specially when I was sick."

"It's definitely not on the menu, but I can order the ingredients to make one."

"Get enough for two. Just talking about them is starting to make me feel real hungry."

I laughed. "Now that is what I want to hear.

«—»

After an hour, Alicia, José and Sandy returned. We still had the rest of the morning to kill before we needed to leave for the airport. Sandy suggested a card game that helped pass the time.

But Nadine had a hard time concentrating. She turned to Alicia. "Should I start getting ready? I know it's still early. But I don't mind."

Alicia placed her cards face-down. "I'm like you. Why put off to the last minute, right?"

Nadine agreed with a fervent nod.

I could see that she needed to be doing something productive rather than twiddling her thumbs.

Alicia began applying the putty to her nose and chin, sculpting with her fingertips and the help of a small tool.

The rest of us watched in such fascination that Nadine squirmed under the scrutiny.

Alicia had to ask her to hold as still as possible.

I turned to the others. "Let's finish our card game so we quit making Nadine so nervous."

We went back to the game, leaving Alicia to work her magic, but José and Sandy couldn't keep from glancing over at the progress.

"Now it's time for the clothes," Alicia said a few minutes later, stepping back and gesturing with a sweep of her arm.

Nadine hopped up, gathered the new outfit into her arms, disappeared into the bathroom and returned wearing a white peasant blouse and long cotton skirt in shades of blue with a paisley print. Her short dyed-brown hair was perfect for the large hoop earrings Sandy selected. A long strand of blue lapis beads hung from her neck. She walked further into the room, showing us the strappy sandals on her feet.

"Oh, I almost forgot the tattoo!" Alicia reached into her bag and pulled out a temporary tattoo of a butterfly. "For your ankle."

Nadine raised her skirt as she placed her foot on the edge of the bed so Alicia could apply the tattoo. "I love it!" Nadine admired the artwork. "It's perfect. I love butterflies."

José spoke up. "You look so different."

Nadine chuckled. "Yeah, don't I? Huge change from the club."

Sandy looked at me, then at Nadine, then back at me. "Wow, you two actually look like mother and daughter. Good job, Alicia."

Alicia beamed with pride as Nadine turned to look in the mirror. She gazed at herself, then at the reflection of me as I stepped to her side.

Nadine grinned. "Hi, Mom!"

I laughed and hugged her.

《—》

The lighter mood in the room kept us uplifted for the rest of the morning. But our van was significantly quieter during the ride to the airport. Nadine sat in the back with Alicia and me while José was in the driver's seat and Sandy was riding shotgun.

Feeling Nadine's nervousness growing with each passing minute, I turned to her. "The good thing about fear is that it keeps us on our toes. We will walk into the terminal holding hands just like a mother and daughter would do. If you see somebody from the club or someone you know, don't panic. Squeeze my hand and nod in their direction."

"Okay." Her eyes widened.

"I know doing so is hard but try to relax and look happy."

She took a deep breath and smiled. "Real enough?" she asked.

Alicia piped in, "Very convincing."

"I've had a lot of practice."

She couldn't have spoken truer words. "Here." I gave her my sunglasses. "Wear these so nobody can see your eyes."

She hesitated then jiggled the glasses. "I could wear them until I get to the gate and give them back to you."

"You can give them back to me when I see you in a couple

of weeks."

As we entered the parking lot, Pete's Bronco was behind us, pulling into the space next to ours. He signaled thumbs up to José. The two men had already discussed the plan, which José had conveyed to us. Pete would hang back as usual and keep an eye on us in the crowd.

Nadine climbed out of the van with her suitcase, and José reached to take it.

She waved him off. "I can carry my own bag, José, thank you."

"You are supposed to look as if you are with your mother. Unless all of you have a bag, you will appear to be traveling alone, which we want to avoid."

I added, "Good point, José. Nadine can take the bag from you at the gate before she boards the plane."

She conceded, handing him the carry-on. After she released it, her anxiety escalated. Sweat beaded on her forehead.

I took both her hands in mine. "Listen to me, Nadine. Stop looking all around. That behavior makes you look suspicious."

"I'm sorry. I can't help it. I'm scared to death."

"We'll wait until you feel ready."

She took a shaky breath. "Okay, I'm ready."

But she didn't sound ready, and I hesitated next to the van. The plan relied on Nadine's ability to act as a tourist.

Sandy slipped her arm around Nadine's elbow. "Pretend you and I are typical bored teenagers being dragged all over this godforsaken country by our crazy hippie mothers looking for merchandise for their head shop in L.A."

Nadine let out a bark of laughter. Alicia and I joined her.

José scratched his head with a bemused expression on his face.

Sandy seemed pleased with herself. "Now you're ready."

I released her left hand but kept a hold of her right. "Let's go."

José and Alicia took the lead. Halfway across the parking lot, I didn't need to look back to know Pete now followed us. I felt his energy.

Inside the terminal, we headed toward the ticket counter to check in and get a boarding pass for Nadine. Suddenly, she tightened her grip around my fingers so hard and almost made me gasp with pain.

"Oh, sweet Jesus, it's Alex." Her panicky whisper was so low I had to strain to hear. Her hand made a slight jerk to the left.

I discreetly checked the direction she indicated. "White shirt, black slacks, against the wall?"

"He's from the club."

"He's not paying you any attention. Remember he's looking for a young girl with long blonde hair, not one with short brown hair." I intentionally swung our hands, hoping to relax her.

Sandy chimed in, "Or with dark skin and a new nose."

Nadine smiled. "Don't forget the butterfly tattoo."

"Of course not." Sandy bumped her shoulder against Nadine in a friendly little nudge. "Next time I see you, I'll take you to get a real one."

"Really?" Nadine's voice squeaked.

"Sure. I might even get one to match. You know, to remember our little adventure together."

"Remember? How could I ever forget?"

I knew Sandy was keeping up the light banter to help Nadine relax. Not only was her ploy working, but it also made them seem like two talkative teenagers. Nadine didn't even realize that their conversation kept her face turned toward Sandy and away from the man from the club.

Together, we approached the counter as if we were all traveling together. I had been carrying Nadine's passport and ticket so she wouldn't be seen getting them out of her purse.

The airline clerk checked the photo, looked at Nadine, then at me. We both smiled benignly. The woman glanced at the rest of our entourage, cocked one eyebrow but otherwise kept her thoughts to herself. Silently, she was thinking we were just another batch of crazy American tourists.

"Do you have any bags to check?" she finally asked.

Nadine and I both answered, "No."

A few moments later, we were on our way toward the gate. This time, Alicia and Sandy walked together ahead of Nadine and me while José followed.

"You'll wait with me until I board, right?" Nadine asked, her hand still clasping mine.

"Yes. We aren't leaving the gate until your plane is in the air. If that man you called Alex is still watching the entrance to the terminal, he will not be able to reach you by the time we walk by him again."

"What if he notices you from earlier and realizes your daughter isn't with you?"

"All the better, Sweetheart," I said gently. "That's what happens at airports. We drop people off and leave alone."

Thirty minutes later, Nadine boarded the plane without incident. When the four of us left the airport, we spotted Alex still standing against the wall. He looked at every person who entered the airport terminal.

Nadine had escaped from right under his nose.

"Good job, Alicia!" I gave her a high five as we walked back to the van. Now if we could just find Faye and have such a successful outcome, I'd be a happy investigator.

«——»

Around five o'clock, Kitty called our hotel room from a payphone at LAX. Nadine had arrived and was processed through customs without difficulty, thanks to Nick, who had taken preemptive measures.

In addition to buying thrift shop furnishings for the apartment, Kitty borrowed household items from the storage locker Lisa had acquired before leaving the Los Angeles area. The entire household of her parents' home had been too much to face after their deaths so Lisa had movers pack it all into boxes and store it. Kitty located pots, pans, linens, and dishes for Nadine to use.

Kitty couldn't talk any longer because Nick's time was limited before his next shift. Nadine called out from the background with a big thank you.

"Tell her I said, 'You're welcome'." I thanked my daughter for all her work, especially on such short notice. "And tell Nick and Ryan 'thanks' for their help, too. Oh, and Michael! We'll have a celebration when we return. I love you."

"I love you, too, Mom."

Alicia answered a knock at our door.

José came into the room. "Ricardo called me. He has information on the investigation team that began in Cancun. He wants us to meet up with them in Guatemala."

CHAPTER 16

August 28, 1990
Tuesday, 6:00 a.m.

The late August morning was already warm, nearly eighty, with some clouds in the sky. Pete waited for us when we stepped out of the elevator in the parking garage. We had a two-day trip ahead of us with plans to stop for the night in Tehuantepec, located on the Pacific Ocean side of the narrow isthmus.

"I restocked our food supplies in the van," Pete said. "We'll make time for rest stops along the way, but no picturesque picnics at any isolated stretches of the road."

José nodded, and then looked at the rest of us. "*Banditos* stake out the places where foreign tourists stop and look around."

"*Banditos?*" Sandy laughed nervously. "You're joking."

"No, he's not," Pete answered. "These aren't cartoon characters like Frito Bandito. These are ruthless criminals who will target anyone."

Her jovial mood vanished.

Alicia waved a hand toward the vehicles. "We can talk all we want in the car. We need to get going."

As we headed south on the busy two-lane highway, Sandy

turned to José, "Do we really need to be afraid of being robbed?"

"You always need to be alert and aware of your surroundings, especially in a foreign country."

Her gaze narrowed. "You didn't answer my question."

I felt her escalating anxiety. "Sandy, there is no immediate fear for our safety. We have Pete keeping an eye out for any suspicious activity."

"Plus, he's armed," Alicia added. "We'll be fine."

"Let me give you a little bit of advice. I depend a lot on my body to warn me if there's something to fear. When I get a sinking feeling in the pit of my stomach, I know someone is trying to exert power over me. Pay attention to those signals. Listen to your inner voice, instead of relying on another person to tell you whether or not to be afraid."

"Sometimes, though, I get scared for no apparent reason."

"When that happens, I always ask myself 'Is the fear real?' My grandmother once told me fear is the only thing that limits a person. The fear itself is paralyzing. I also ask myself, 'What is the worst thing that can happen?'"

With a flip of her hand in the air, Sandy answered, "We could be shot by *banditos!*"

"Being afraid of that happening isn't going to help" I said. "In fact, those kinds of thoughts put more energy out to the universe to manifest your worst fear. It's better to let go of the negativity, stay alert and enjoy the day."

Alicia nodded. "Well said."

"Well, if you two are playing it cool, I suppose I can, too." Sandy turned back around in her passenger seat and gazed out the window.

I could sense that her fear-energy had dropped considerably.

We took Federal Highway 200 south from Acapulco toward the state of Oaxaca. Known as *Carretera Costera*, the two-lane road followed the Pacific coastline, winding in and out of small towns and farms. With the temperature rising, I was grateful for our air-conditioned van so we could keep the windows closed and avoid the heavy exhaust fumes from the traffic.

We made a few rest stops along the way, locations determined by Pete. We could never be too careful. To keep up the appearance of being store owners, we shopped for an hour in Puerto Escondido, purchasing the regional folk art called *alebrijes*—miniature woodcarvings of brightly colored imaginary creatures. We welcomed the opportunity to stretch our legs and have lunch under a shady canopy of trees along the beach.

By 1 p.m., José was eager to get going. He wanted us to be in Tehuantepec before dark. The remaining distance was only two hundred sixty-nine kilometers, a little over one hundred sixty-seven miles. If there were no delays caused by traffic, he expected the rest of our drive to take about three hours. If so, we'd reach our destination long before sunset.

José was hired to be our driver because he knew how to get around Mexico like no one else. He explained how quickly a rainstorm could wash out a road that could take weeks to repair. A three-hour trip could take twelve hours, or longer. Even though there had not been any significant rain storms in recent days, and none predicted, we could never be too careful.

Fortunately, we didn't encounter any washouts, but we did sit, with dozens of other cars, after a large delivery truck lost a rear wheel. Sandy expressed concern that it was a staged by the *banditos* mentioned earlier.

José said *banditos* were not likely behind a break-down during the day with too many witnesses who might also be carrying their own weapons for protection. Thieves would strike in the middle of the night or on a deserted road, or both.

Directly behind us in his Bronco, Pete got out and walked toward the driver's window of the van. From the way he acted, he could have been any other stranded motorist and not someone we knew. He chatted amicably with José who cut the engine to save fuel.

I unbuckled my seatbelt and slid open the side door.

Sandy jumped out and stretched, gazing at the thick bushes and trees lining the highway. The afternoon sun was hot. The inside of the van would soon be sweltering. Even if venturing toward the canopy of shade had been safe, the dense vegetation kept us on the shoulder of the road.

Before the situation became too desperate, we were finally on our way again. Ninety minutes later, we arrived in the city of Tehuantepec— "Hill of the Wild Animals"—named by the Aztecs for the ferocious native Zapotec warriors.

Alicia admired the brightly-colored blouses and flowing skirts on the tall, dark, smooth-skinned women who walked with a graceful presence.

Sandy asked, "Where are the men?"

José told us about the unique matriarchal society where

men, outnumbered five to one, stay home or work the fields. For centuries, the Zapotec region of Oaxaca has been known for independent women in the male-dominated country. The area is also a safe haven for homosexuals who are not welcome in other areas of Mexico that are strongly influenced by the Catholic Church.

José recited other historical facts as he maneuvered the busy streets. In a short while, he turned a corner with a ten-foot stone wall on our right. A moment later, we stopped in front of tall, ornate wrought-iron gates. A brass plate mounted on the wall read: *Villa Ortega.*

Sandy's head swiveled as she asked José. "Is this your place?"

"The house belongs to my whole family. We spend the holidays here. My parents have a home in Mexico City, but my father is now semi-retired so they come here more often." He tapped twice on the horn.

A uniformed guard came into view and waved while the gates slowly retracted on metal tracks embedded in the cobblestone driveway.

I'm sure I wasn't the only one in the van gaping slack-jawed at the resort-like residence. Pete followed us inside and the gate closed behind his SUV. The white two-story house was a Spanish colonial with a terra-cotta tile roof, almost hidden by climbing mounds of red bougainvillea that also draped from eaves and archways.

The front door opened. A tall, older woman stepped out, a wide smile on her face.

José waved, explaining to us that Guadalupe had worked

for his family for as long as he could remember, and everyone called her *Tia* Lupe.

Her black hair, lightly threaded with strands of gray, was pulled back into a thick braid. She had thick brows and an aristocratic nose. Similar to the other women we had seen on our way through town, she wore a white blouse embroidered in red, yellow and orange flowers, and a skirt of intricate patchwork.

José gave her a warm embrace, speaking to her in the indigenous Zapotec dialect that was close enough to my knowledge of Spanish I did not have difficulty understanding his introduction of each of us.

She firmly shook our hands, repeating our names as José had recited them. *"Llámeme Tía Lupe, por favor. Ven conmigo."* *Call me Aunt Lupe , please. Come with me.*

With a sweep of her hand, she gestured to follow her. As she led us to our rooms on the second floor, she told us that dinner would be served in twenty minutes, giving us time to freshen up.

Alicia, Sandy, Pete and I met in the hallway and walked down the stairs, remarking about the delicious aromas, and we found José waiting to escort us into the dining room. Two tall silver candelabras illuminated the linen-covered table set with fine china and crystal goblets. Serving dishes of all sizes filled the surface of a massive wooden sideboard. The meal was more like a feast for royalty.

Sandy spoke in a light tone about staying behind in the lap of luxury while the rest of us continued our mission to find Faye. Despite the gravity of our missing person case, everyone should maintain some equilibrium, and levity helped a great deal.

CHAPTER 17

August 29, 1990
Wednesday, 6:45 a.m.

The next morning, I awoke to the smell of fried bacon. I quickly dressed and headed down the hall to the bathroom, bumping into Alicia as she was coming out.

"Is everyone up?" I asked.

"Pete and José are already downstairs," she said. "Sandy is still in bed. I'll knock on her door."

A few minutes later, I was still moving slowly, craving a jumpstart of caffeine.

Alicia, José and Pete sat at the kitchen table, all three with cups of coffee. *Tia* Lupe patted a corn mixture into tortillas, cooking them on a large griddle alongside sizzling bacon strips and crumbled *chorizo*.

They were talking and laughing. I love the sound of laughter.

Tia Lupe wiped her hands so she could pour coffee for me, but I insisted I could do it myself.

Within minutes, Sandy shuffled into the kitchen, sleepy-eyed and barely awake.

José waited until we finished eating before he got down to business, preparing us for our travel into Guatemala. Like

Mexico, violent crime was a serious concern due to endemic poverty, an abundance of weapons and dysfunctional law enforcement and judicial systems. Uncontrolled drug and alien smuggling made the Guatemalan border with Mexico particularly dangerous. Rumors were rampant about child stealing and murder for organ harvesting.

As usual, Pete would be following us. Carlos Rios and Elegio Garcia, the two Mexican Intelligent officers we'd met in Ricardo's office, would meet us in Guatemala City. Sandy had not been in on that initial meeting so I quickly explained, they were searching other parts of the country for information that would lead us to Faye Franklin.

After I finished, José continued with his warnings. He told us to avoid contact with children, which would arouse suspicion. The slightest misstep could cause panic and violence. He and Pete had already discussed their plans to steer clear of areas where demonstrations were occurring or where crowds may appear to be agitated.

He watched Sandy shift nervously in her chair.

"I am sorry to make you worry again, but Guatemala has the most violent crime in all of Latin America. Criminals know there is little chance they will get caught."

"Are they targeting Americans?" she asked.

"Not specifically. They are not selective. They will approach anyone with anything of value. They take jewelry, purses, wallets and luggage. As long as they don't encounter any problems, they usually leave without hurting anyone. That does not mean they will not hesitate to shoot."

Pete rested a forearm on the table. "Carlos and Elegio are

waiting at a hotel with the highest security. They also have a car so whenever we are out in public, they'll take the lead position with the van in the middle."

We hurriedly finished our breakfast, took showers, and were ready to leave in forty-five minutes.

We walked toward the van, and *Tia* Lupe caught up with us and gave us two brown paper sacks of food to take along on our trip.

"Tia Lupe, thank you for everything. If you come to the U.S., please know you are always welcome at my home. I am not as good of a cook, but we will make sure you are comfortable." I gave *Tia* Lupe a hug and we were on our way.

«——»

Nine hours later, after only a few brief rest stops, we arrived in Guatemala City at half past five and noticed the emaciated street-children wearing torn and dirty rags, such a sharp contrast to the colorfully dressed women of Tehuantepec. In a city of one and a half million people, nine out of ten families lived in poverty. Unable to feed their children, parents abandoned them to survive on their own. Amnesty International estimated five thousand children roamed the city, most turning to theft, prostitution and sniffing cobbler's glue to deal with the hunger pangs.

Seeing so many kids in such dire circumstances had a sobering effect on all of us, particularly Sandy. Usually perched on the edge of her seat, pointing at something or other and asking José about it, she became quiet.

My chest ached with the sadness, the desperation of it all.

Alicia voiced what all of us were thinking—if only we could help them.

In stark contrast, The Westin Camino Real was a luxury hotel in the high-end area known as *Zona* 10, also considered the safest neighborhood. After we checked into our rooms, we gathered together in José's room to wait for the government intelligence agents.

Seeing them arrive, Sandy's eyes widened and she sat upright.

I knew she found them attractive. I had to admit they were as handsome as any male models I had ever seen.

Leaning close, she whispered in my ear, "Can I ride with them?"

José introduced her to Carlos Rios and Elegio Garcia. Both were equally charming in their attentiveness to Sandy which did not go unnoticed by José, who cleared his throat.

She turned to him with a dreamy crooked smile. "Yes?"

"Ricardo sent Carlos and Elegio to Cancun and another team to Brazil."

She looked at the two agents. "Why Brazil?"

"That is where this group of clubs ends," Elegio said, then directed his attention to the group. "If Faye is to be sold, she would be auctioned off in Brazil."

"What did you learn in Cancun?" I asked.

"Carlos and I made friends with one of the security guards, Chico, at the club in Cancun. One night, we took him out on the town to loosen him up, see if he'd talk. After a few Zombies, he got real chatty about the girls at the club and the club's activities. We couldn't inquire specifically about Faye without raising suspicion. So, Elegio asked about getting a pretty young blonde for the night."

"No blondes were working at the club," Elegio explained. "So I thought if I asked about one, then Chico might hook me up with Faye or someone who might have seen her. He told me I was wasting my time when there were plenty of other girls to choose from."

Carlos added, "Just when we thought we hit a dead end, we heard Chico mention a blonde American named Faye. The other girls talked about her being sent to the farm in Nicaragua after she tried to escape."

My senses heightened, further proving I was right about the significance of this farm. But were we too late? She'd already been sent away. Something was off but I couldn't pinpoint it.

"Was Chico able to supply the location?" Alicia asked, clearly excited that there was a connection to their own information.

"Only that it is on the east coast on the Caribbean. And accessed only by boat."

José raised his hand. "Ricardo already has two other investigators on the ground in Nicaragua. He is waiting to hear back from them. I was instructed to check in with him as soon as all of us were together." He reached for his portable phone to make the call.

"Just how many people are looking for Faye?" Sandy asked me.

"As many as Ricardo needs," I said. "Her parents are willing to pay for an entire army, if that's what it takes to bring their daughter home."

A few moments later, José contacted Ricardo, then handed me the phone. After an exchange of greetings and confirming we were all fine, I listened intently so I could relay everything to the rest of my group.

According to the other investigators in Nicaragua, Faye had been at the farm described by Chico, the Cancun security guard. After trying to escape, she was told any further lack of cooperation would result in the death of her family in America. She was given heavy doses of drugs and raped repeatedly by her captors, who sexually abused her more than the other girls.

Unfortunately, the agents missed her by two days. She had already been taken away, heading to Cartagena, Columbia by boat with two other young women and several children.

Ricardo finished with a heavy sigh. "After you tell everyone what I have just told you, please find out if any of them wish to go home. Rios, Garcia and Young are trained to deal with the danger ahead. The others, I am not so confident."

My entire body felt the impact of his news as if I had been knocked off my feet from an explosive blast of hot air. I should have been elated that we finally had confirmation that Faye had in fact been kidnapped and that she was still alive. Instead, I was reeling from the sadness and disappointment, wishing I could have connected and saved her before she had been transported so far away. And I was scared. More scared than I had ever been in my entire life. Columbia was far more dangerous than Mexico or anywhere else. I feared for Faye. For my team. And, yes, even for myself.

"Let me talk to them, and I'll call you back." I hung up the phone, feeling depleted.

Hearing the information made the group fall silent. I looked at each person in the room. Ricardo was right about Carlos, Elegio and Pete. All were stoic with an air of determination to move forward and move quickly. José, Alicia and Sandy were trying to be brave while battling their fear of the unknown. "Does anyone want to go home?" I asked.

Sandy gave a furtive glance at me, then Alicia, and finally José.

He watched Sandy with worry in his eyes. "No," he said. "I want to go on."

Alicia straightened her shoulders. "Me, too."

I rested my hand on Sandy's arm. In my mind's eye, I saw flashes of her thoughts, memories of her abusive past. "Sandy, it's okay if you need to go home. I understand. We all understand."

She shook her head. "I want to help. I don't think I could live with myself if I didn't stay and try to find Faye."

I didn't need to ask the three men where they stood. And I was sure they would be insulted if I did. "Then it's settled. Ricardo wanted to make sure we were all still on board before he gave me further instructions. I'll call him back right now, and then we can finalize our next step."

After speaking with him again, I laid out the plan to the others. "Pete, Carlos and Elegio will drive the van to Cartagena while the rest of us take a plane. José, we still need you to act as if you are the hired guide for the three women on a buying trip for our store. The four of us will take the disguises, make-up, portable phones and our bags. The rest goes in the van. Make sure your passport is available, safe and concealed on your body."

"Wouldn't it be safer to stick together?" Sandy asked, with an all-encompassing wave of her hand, then a jerk of her thumb toward the two agents and Pete. "I'd feel safer with them close than going anywhere without them. No offense, José."

"None taken." Shaking his head, José held up his palms. "I agree wholeheartedly."

"They will arrive at the hotel about the same time as we do," I said, "if they take turns driving through the night, which will be dangerous but not as much as having us along. They also have government identification from Mexico. There is a flight to Columbia day after tomorrow from here. Ricardo will book the tickets and send them by courier. He'll also make sure we are registered at the U.S. Embassy in Bogotá. If the US Department receives information on potential threats, they will inform Ricardo."

I sensed Kitty was about to call.

"Please excuse me for a moment. My daughter needs to talk to me."

José turned with an upraised eyebrow. "I didn't hear your phone."

"Don't you know Deanne is telepathic?" Sandy said with a grin.

He gave her a wary look, then turned to me. "Is that true?"

"Yes. I hadn't meant for Sandy to reveal this information. On the other hand, it was bound to come out sooner or later. "I can send and receive communication, but I need to speak in person to get the details."

"How does it work?" he asked. "Do you know what I am thinking now?"

I turned and looked at him, gauging his intent. "Only that you're curious. I don't know the details of why you are curious. Telepathic communication is brief and needs an emotion strong enough to push it to me. You are definitely a Sender, as most people are, often without realizing they are. Can you receive?"

"I don't know." He lifted his brows with a bit of inward wonder.

I smiled, sensing his openness to the idea of exploring his own psychic abilities. "We are all born with ESP to some degree. I will be happy to talk more another time. Right now, I need to call my daughter. I'll be back in a few minutes."

After learning from Kitty about a plumbing problem at my house and giving her the go-ahead for the plumber, I chatted briefly until I received a distinct feeling that I needed to act upon right away.

"Faye's parents need to meet you in Columbia," she said matter-of-factly.

I accepted how Kitty had picked up on the same thing. "Yes, that's exactly what I just got. And they need to bring antibiotics." I wanted to reach across the miles to give my daughter a hug. She sent me the telepathic image of hugging me back. I love when that happens. "I've got to contact Ricardo to make the arrangements immediately. I'll call you soon. Love you!"

"Love you, too, Mom!"

When I returned to the room, I saw that Pete, Elegio and

Carlos had left. Alicia, Sandy and José were playing a game of cards.

"I got a 'hit' that we will find Faye," I said to them. "And I feel her parents need to be there."

CHAPTER 18

August 31, 1990
Friday, 9:00 a.m.

The trunk of the twenty-year-old green taxi was big enough to hold our bags while Alicia, Sandy and I took the back seat and José slid into the front passenger seat. On the way to La Aurora International Airport, he chatted in Spanish with the middle-aged driver, weaving a lighthearted story about his work as a guide and helping us find crafts for my fictitious boutique.

My mind wandered to Pete, Carlos and Elegio who had left the previous morning in the van after Pete dropped off his Bronco in the US Embassy parking lot. I felt no sense of imminent danger, which allowed me to relax a little bit. But I couldn't say the same about Sandy.

"Do you want to go home?" I asked under my breath for only her to hear.

"No, why do you ask?"

"I sense you're afraid."

"I am afraid, but I still want to go."

"Okay. Just checking before we leave for Columbia."

《—》

After the two-hour flight, I was startled to see soldiers carrying rifles at the modern airport in Cartagena. "José, do you think something has happened to bring all these soldiers to the airport?"

"No. Ricardo is on top of this, and he would advise us if there was a problem. I am looking for the young man who will take us to our hotel."

"I see a good-looking young man headed toward us."

"Sandy is falling into lust again."

We chuckled.

"Hola. Estoy Arturo. Estoy buscando para José Ortega."

José identified himself, then asked in Spanish, "What is the password?"

"Verdad es oro." Truth is gold.

"Sí. Mui bien." He turned to introduce us to Arturo.

We each shook his hand and followed our driver to the car. During the slow drive to our hotel, José was once again in the front passenger seat. This time, however, he did not try to entertain with imaginative tales. The topic was the political and military state of the country.

Arturo knew our reasons for being there and held back nothing. "Keep a close eye on this girl," he said in Spanish, not using Sandy's name so she did not become alarmed. Alicia and I could understand every word. "She is exactly the type of person the traffickers are looking to find. She is young and attractive. The lucrative returns from drugs and kidnapping dominate this society. Street children don't have a chance here."

"I understand journalists are also targeted," I said in his

native language.

"That's right," Arturo answered, glancing at me in his rearview mirror with wrinkled brows. "There have been threats against *Americanos* in Columbia. The embassy strongly encourages caution and to remain vigilant. Remember, firearms are prevalent here, and any altercation can turn violent."

"Will we be safe?" Alicia asked.

"I was told by Ricardo you three women are to remain in the hotel and keep a very low profile. The city is relatively safe, depending upon the time of day and the location. Outside the city—" He shook his head. "Extremely dangerous. No one is immune from being kidnapped. Your U.S. government places a high priority on the safe return of its citizens. Unfortunately, their policy is to *not* make concessions or strike a deal with kidnappers, so their help is limited. That is why the Franklins sought the help of investigators from the private sector."

We pulled up in front of the hotel where armed soldiers stood near the entrance, close enough to intimidate but far enough away from the doorway to allow people to pass. I felt a knot in my stomach. The danger was real. I love the work I do, but there are times when I know my life could be threatened. Time to focus.

Arturo insisted on helping José carry our bags to the front desk to check in, suggesting the rest of us wait in the cafe on the other side of the lobby.

"Here I will say good-bye and wish you success," he said. "If you need anything, you can call the telephone number I will leave with your guide." He gave a wink and a grin.

Alicia, Sandy and I thanked him and wandered to the small

hotel restaurant decorated in bright tropical colors. After we ordered lunch, including something for José, we grew quiet, listening to the conversations of tourists around us.

José caught up with us a short while later, his portable phone strap over his shoulder. "I sent our things up to our rooms. Mine is next to yours again. But yours is a two-room suite with a bedroom and a living room that has a convertible sofa. I ordered a portable bed, too. None of the others has checked in. From the upstairs room, I will call Ricardo. I don't want to have a conversation here where someone might hear me."

We couldn't agree more, as we had already discovered that to be true. So the four of us chatted through our mid-day meal as if we were part of a sightseeing excursion and waiting for the rest of our party to arrive.

«—»

Twenty minutes after José left us at the door of our hotel room, he returned to inform us the team members coming from Nicaragua, Juan and Caesar, were following up on some leads about Faye being held outside the city. "Ricardo told them we arrived safely and gave them my room number."

"Any word from Pete, Carlos and Elegio?" I asked.

Sitting cross-legged on the rollaway bed, Sandy paused in her game of solitaire. Her interest piqued by the names of the two cute intelligent agents.

"They have been delayed. All I know is that they stopped to help a family who had been jumped by *banditos*."

Wide-eyed, Sandy crushed the cards to her chest. "Is

everyone okay?"

José nodded. "I assume so, or they would not have continued their trip. I'm sure we will get the details when they arrive."

"Now I'm glad we didn't go with them." Her shoulders slumped. "Flying *is* safer."

I looked out our window at the city sprawled out below us with too many casinos to count. The conversation in the car about politics and crime came flooding back. Arturo had been outspoken about the recession crippling the city.

Through my research done in the states, I learned Cartagena had been the safe haven of drug lords who were heavily invested in the popular tourist area of Bocagrande, a narrow peninsula on the east side of the city, capitalizing on the white sand beaches and the blue Caribbean Sea. Until a year ago, Cartagena was off-limits for drug trafficking and killings. The same could not be said for *human* trafficking in the sex trade, which thrives on the multitude of foreign tourists.

Then, the previous September, the Hotel Cartagena Hilton was bombed, killing two doctors attending a medical convention. Minutes later, a car bomb exploded, injuring several people. In November, a shopping center on the city's south side was bombed. Tourism plummeted. American cruise ships no longer made Cartagena a port of call. European flights dwindled.

In January, Columbian cocaine traffickers declared a truce in their war. In February, President Bush's anti-drug summit with three South American presidents was held in Cartagena. His visit was for only a few hours and was held in a high-security military location outside the city, but the message conveyed to the media was the return of peace and tranquility, and, most of all safety for Americans and other foreign travelers. Despite the positive P.R., there was still a high level of risk, as Arturo had pointed out.

Sandy had not followed the conversation in Spanish, and I had not yet conveyed the recent history of the city to her. She was still very new to the tedium of an investigation and not accustomed to sitting around a hotel room, waiting for action. I could sense her restlessness.

She finished another round of solitaire with a heavy sigh, scooping up the cards. "José, couldn't we go out for a while? I need to stretch my legs. You could bring your portable telephone in case anyone wanted to reach us."

Mouth pinched tight, he shook his head. "We are to stay in our rooms until the entire team is here."

She popped up from the bed and started pacing. "What is the big deal? What could happen with soldiers on every corner? They are doing their job so people like us can move around the city, right? I just feel so amped up with adrenaline with no place to go."

Alicia chuckled. "You will need to learn how to relax if you expect to make a living as an investigator."

"Sometimes," I said, "you have to wait for the correct information or for the right time to proceed with your case."

"I like the moving forward," she said with frank honesty. "Not the delays in between."

"Patience takes practice," Alicia added. "Not everyone is good at it. I bring a book to read during the down time. But even I have my limits. I have to admit I do not take surveillance work because there is just too much waiting for something to happen. And forget bathroom breaks!"

"What? How?"

Alicia laughed. "*That* is a problem. For us girls, that is. Guys have it easy. Right, José?"

He held up his hands, palms out. "No comment."

"You can't look for a restroom," I added, "especially if your subject has been spotted. You might miss him leaving the area while you were gone for a few minutes."

"Have you ever done surveillance?" Sandy asked me.

"Yes, but for short periods of time. I did not have to follow the subject of the surveillance. I have a good team of men who get results about ninety-five percent of the time."

Suddenly, José's beeper began chirping. He looked down at the readout as he shut it off. "It's Ricardo. I left my portable phone in my room. Do you mind if we use yours?"

"Of course not. Be my guest."

A few moments later, after he reached Ricardo, his face lit up. Covering the receiver with a hand, he whispered, "They located Faye!"

CHAPTER 19

Sandy and Alicia whooped with joy as the three of us jumped to our feet and hugged each other in celebration. José hushed us so he could hear Ricardo on the other end of the line. We contained our excitement until he was off the phone.

"Caesar and Juan found the compound next to a river in the jungle, but it is in a bad area. Right in the middle of land owned by rival drug cartels. The region is very unstable. Our men found an old barn that overlooks the place with children outside. They saw a young blonde woman with another girl picking plants by the river. Caesar snuck down to the water and identified Faye. She wouldn't leave without the other girl, so they are bringing her back, too."

I sighed and kept my feelings to myself. This made our situation more complicated. I did not want to put negative energy into the situation. I needed to get all the details before I could make any plans for our escape. I reminded myself I was not alone and not to allow fear to run me. I took several deep breaths and relaxed before I asked José, "Any word on Faye's parents?"

"They arrive by private plane tomorrow."

"And Pete's team?"

"They should be here soon. Ricardo said the trip from Guatemala City was hell."

"While we wait, we should use this time to prepare for Faye's arrival. We don't know what her condition might be, but we can't risk taking her to a clinic. Both girls will need food. And clothes. Let me make a list." I reached for my purse but my mouth and throat suddenly felt hot and painful. I winced.

"Deanne?" Alicia touched my elbow. "What's wrong? Are you okay?"

I stroked my fingers down my throat and swallowed, though it was difficult. For a brief moment, my tongue felt too thick to talk. The sensations vanished as quickly as they had appeared. I cleared my throat, swallowing easily. "I'm fine now."

Sandy tilted her head, her forehead creased. "What was that all about?"

I gave a half-hearted smile. "We need broth and clear liquids. One or both of the girls will have a hard time eating solid food."

"Add it to the list," Alicia said, then volunteered to go with José to the market while Sandy and I waited for Pete and the others.

After they left, I turned to Sandy. "How about a game of poker?

"No. I don't have any money."

"We'll play for peanuts. I'm sure I have some left in my bag."

She laughed. "Are you always so prepared?"

"Of course."

I enjoyed Sandy's energy. She was a good sender of telepathic messages. She would be fun to teach how to receive messages. We played cards until José and Alicia returned with two bags of groceries, as well as some first aid items I had starred on the list.

They had not been back more than a few minutes when we heard a knock on the door. José went to the door but didn't open it. "Who is it?"

"Pete."

José quickly unlocked the door and stepped back, allowing the three men to enter our hotel room. All appeared as though they had just stepped out of a shower. Their hair was wet, and their cheeks were clean-shaven. They wore rumpled but clean clothes. And they all looked completely and utterly exhausted.

"How about some coffee?" I offered. "We could order room service or use the packets supplied by housekeeping."

Carlos waved me off. "Water will be fine, thanks. I need sleep, not caffeine."

"Me, too," added Elegio.

Pete rubbed his neck wearily. "Make that three."

I urged them to sit as Sandy and José brought glasses of water. Elegio and Carlos chose the edge of the convertible couch, expressing gratitude for the water. Pete thanked José for the glass and took a long sip of water before settling into a chair. Sandy plopped on the rollaway. Alicia, José and I remained standing.

"Ricardo said you stopped to help a family on the road," José said.

Carlos dropped his gaze and leaned forward, his elbows on his knees, holding the glass between his hands. Elegio shook his head, his mouth in a grim line.

Pete took a deep breath and blew it out hard. "Hell of a mess," he said. "A family from Sweden had a flat tire on their rental car. The father got out to fix it when a truck stopped behind them. He thought they would offer to help. Instead, they gang-raped his wife in front of him and his two children."

Beside me, Alicia cupped her hand to her mouth, stifling a gasp.

"¡Dios Mío!" José squeezed his eyes shut and hung his head, crossing himself in the sign of the crucifix.

"The banditos took everything, including the car, leaving the family huddled by the side of the road. We were out in the middle of nowhere when I spotted them ahead on the highway. In the distance, the object looked like a carcass of a cow or some other big animal. When I slowed the car as we approached, I realized there was a man sitting on the shoulder of the road with a woman curled up in his lap and a kid clinging to each of his sides."

I heard Sandy sniffling. I glanced at her and saw tears ran down her cheeks. Only then did I feel my own and wiped them away.

"I pulled over before I got too close so we wouldn't scare them. The three of us approached with our hands up to show we had no weapons and meant no harm. The two little kids had wet their pants and were sobbing uncontrollably. The wife was glassy-eyed and catatonic, wrapped in her husband's shirt. Her face, arms and legs were bloody and dirty. The husband was rocking her and talking in Swedish. He didn't respond to us initially. We thought he didn't speak Spanish or English. He had blood smeared on his chest so we thought he was seriously hurt, too. Turned out to be his wife's blood. Eventually, Elegio got through to the husband. The guy finally started talking to us in English, telling us what happened."

Pete leaned forward, resting his elbows on his knees. "We drove them to the nearest town and stayed with them until we were sure they would get the help they needed. We couldn't stay any longer so I spoke with Ricardo and gave his phone number to the husband in case they required further assistance. I also gave him my number, but I don't know where this case is going so I couldn't do any more than to ask him to call me in a few weeks to let me know they returned home safely."

I sensed Pete's feelings of guilt about not being able to do more for the Swedish family. "Don't beat yourself up. You guys saved them. If you hadn't come along, who knows what would have happened."

He nodded solemnly, as did Elegio and Carlos.

"We had a few other incidents," Elegio said, "but there is no need to recount them."

Carlos nodded. "We are here. We are safe. That is enough talk about it."

Pete remained silent but he glanced at them with a very faint smile and only the slightest tip of his head, acknowledging their humble reticence.

Ricardo had said they had been through hell.

After hearing the one horror story, I could only imagine the rest. Normally, I might have picked up on their thoughts. But all three men had closed that door to their recent past. However, I did feel their exhaustion. Every muscle in my body ached as soon as they walked into our hotel room. I felt as if I could crawl into bed and fall asleep immediately.

Pete looked at José, then me. "When I checked in with Ricardo to let him know we were in our room here at the hotel, he told me Juan and Caesar had Faye and another girl. They are bringing them here later."

"Yes," I said. "After dark."

His nod showed his approval. "Safer that way."

"Yes."

The room fell quiet. Sandy had stopped sniffling. Only the hum of the window air conditioning unit could be heard.

Carlos looked at his wristwatch. "We have a few hours more to get some sleep. I don't know about you two, but I'm going back to our room."

Pete and Elegio stood, handing their glasses back to José.

"We won't be far," Pete said. "We're just down the hall, next to the stairwell."

《—》

At nine-thirty in the evening, all seven of us gathered again in the suite, anxiously awaiting the arrival of Juan and Caesar with the two girls. At nine-forty, José answered the knock at the door.

I think we were all a little disheartened to hear Arturo's voice identifying himself.

José let him in, and he was followed by two girls who looked like they had not bathed in weeks. If the taller blonde was actually Faye Franklin, she was almost unrecognizable. Her eyes were hollow. She had raw sores on her face, arms and hands. Her jaw and neck were slightly swollen and flushed pink as if hot and inflamed. I remembered the tight feeling in my throat earlier.

Behind them stood two men gently but quickly urging the girls out of the hallway and into the safety of the room.

I reached out my hand in greeting but the blonde looked past me, lost in her own world.

The younger, dark-haired girl glanced at my hand, scrubbed her palm on her dirty dress, and shook my hand with a firm grip.

"Hello, I am Lucinda," she said, carefully enunciating each word in a heavy Spanish accent.

"Hola, Lucinda. Mi nombre es Deanne Acuña." As I watched her shoulders relax, I continued in her native tongue. "I am a private investigator. Faye's parents hired me and this team to find her and bring her home. They are on their way here."

Lucinda glanced nervously around the room, her jaw clenched tight. The chatty girl had suddenly become as mute as her friend.

"Do you understand what I said?"

There was no response.

"Are you hungry or thirsty?"

The younger girl nodded.

Alicia beckoned them to the small bistro table with two place settings and a tray of food. "Would you like something to eat?"

Wide-eyed Lucinda took Faye's hand and pulled her toward the table, then gently guided her down into a chair before taking a seat.

The younger girl stuffed cheese and crackers into her

mouth, barely chewing and swallowing before grabbing a slice of apple and a piece of bologna lunchmeat.

When Alicia set a glass of milk in front of her, she guzzled it down, then grabbed a banana and started peeling it.

"How old are you, Lucinda?" I asked, again in Spanish.

"Fourteen. Almost." She placed the banana on Faye's plate, and mashed it with the back of a fork before offering a forkful of the soft food to her silent friend.

"She can't eat?"

The answer came slowly, almost reluctantly. "She has sores in her mouth ... and her, um, privates."

"Faye, are you in pain?" I asked in English but received no answer. I walked closer to her and squatted, looking upward into her dirty face. I tried a different tactic. "*Is* your name Faye Franklin?"

She blinked and looked at Lucinda who swallowed hard, even though nothing was in her mouth.

I suddenly felt a wave of sadness from the dark-haired girl. She was afraid to lose her best friend, afraid of being left behind when Faye's parents came to take her home. I realized this was the reason Lucinda had clammed up after our initial introduction.

Lucinda leaned in close to her friend, stroking her arm, speaking softly but slowly, struggling to translate her native language. "They need to know you are the girl they've been looking for."

Faye lifted her head and met my gaze. Her eyes glistened with tears. One slid down her cheek. She opened her mouth to speak, but her tongue was grotesquely swollen. "I—MMM—

Faye." Drool dripped from her bottom lip. She swallowed and winced. She bowed her head and shook it side to side. "F-fff-WANK-win."

I felt a wave of shame emanating from her and slamming into the center of my chest. All of my maternal instincts rose, and I dropped to my knees on the floor beside her chair then slid my arms around her waist. She melted into my hug, dropping her face to my shoulder and crying deep, gut-wrenching sobs. Ignoring the smell of putrid breath and sour body odor, I stroked her hair.

"Faye, listen to me. We don't care if you can't talk or why." I made sure my voice remained calm, no matter the state of my own feelings. "None of what occurred is your fault. The only thing that matters is that you *survived*. Despite everything that has happened to you, you stayed alive because you are strong. Do you hear me?"

She nodded and gingerly straightened her spine.

My mind filled with violent flashes of her memory that she unknowingly projected telepathically. I hated the grotesque images of assaults. My stomach roiled. Bile rose in my throat.

My God, what this poor girl had suffered! I stroked her cheek to reassure her and felt the heat of infection pulsing from inside her mouth and throat. The antibiotics I had asked her father to bring could not come soon enough. "We will do our best to make you comfortable until your parents get here tomorrow. Do you want to try to eat a little bit and then take a long, hot bath?"

Faye nodded.

Lucinda raised a forkful of banana toward Faye's mouth.

Alicia offered to help but Lucinda politely declined. Her job as caretaker to her best friend was not over as long as she was still around.

I opened a can of beef broth with a can opener Alicia had bought at the store, then poured the broth into the empty coffee pot and turned on the hot plate beneath.

Sandy stepped up next to me, her gaze focused on the table.

I sensed her feelings of helplessness but waited for her to speak.

"Is there anything I can do?"

"Why don't you and José go down to the cafe to get a couple of chocolate milkshakes for the girls? See if they have any applesauce, too."

"I'll ask if they have any other soft foods, too. Maybe some Cream of Wheat?"

"That would be great to order for breakfast tomorrow from room service."

Sandy gave me a small smile, glad she had come up with a good suggestion. "I'll get José to take me downstairs for the shakes."

Sitting only a few feet away, Pete had overheard the conversation. "I think you have everything under control here. I'm feeling like having a late snack. Do you mind if the boys and I tag along to the cafe before we call it a night?"

Sandy didn't miss a beat. She knew darn well they were determined to keep an eye on anyone who left the room. "Sure, we'd love the company."

José glanced at the two government agents who had shoved

themselves to their feet to open the door for Sandy. He gazed at her basking in the glow of attention, then he caught me watching the whole scene.

He scratched his head in a way that made me think of the perplexed expression on Stan Laurel from an old "Laurel and Hardy" comedy. The humor of it all would have escaped him so I simply gave my shoulders a shrug.

With a resigned smile, he said, "I'll say good-night now, but I'll make sure Sandy is back in twenty minutes. Can we bring back anything for either of you?"

"Not for me," Alicia said. "Thanks, anyway."

"Thank you but I'm fine," I answered, grateful for his considerate nature. "Good night, José."

CHAPTER 20

After the door closed, I turned back to the two girls at the table and gestured toward the half-open door leading to the bedroom. "Who wants to bathe first?"

"Faye will," Lucinda offered, "but I have to help her." She took her friend's hand and helped her stand. Faye appeared too weak and unsteady so I stepped to her other side, put my arm around her waist and walked them to bathroom. Alicia had already started filling the tub before we came in. Towels and washcloths were set out. She had also placed toiletries on the vanity.

I picked up a tube of antibiotic ointment from the vanity and showed it to Lucinda. "For the sores on her face and hands."

Lucinda nodded. "Thank you."

Alicia left and returned with a stack of new clothes in her arms. "I hope these will fit. I had to guess what sizes to buy. At the bottom of the stack are nightgowns, too."

Lucinda held up a pink princess t-shirt and smiled. She grabbed the purple shirt and held it up to Faye who looked down at the image of a fairy and managed a little smile of her own. The denim blue jeans were a little too big for them, but Alicia had also purchased skinny belts to cinch the waists. She also gave them each a dark blue sweatshirt with a fairy tale castle on the front. Again, a bit too large. But the fit didn't matter—the items were fresh and clean. Same for the pink and yellow matching nightgowns.

They expressed their gratitude and reverently set the clothing to one side as if they were as precious as gold.

Alicia excused herself and left the bathroom, but I remained. "Lucinda, you look so tired. Are you sure I can't help you with Faye?"

"No, thank you. But we don't mind if you stay. Do we, Faye?"

I did not feel they allowed me to stay because they trusted me. But more like they had become so accustomed to the complete disregard for their privacy that modesty was no longer a consideration.

Faye sat on the closed toilet lid like a limp doll as her young friend squatted to remove dirty brown sneakers that had once been white and had worn-out shoelaces long enough to thread through only a few of the holes and tie in a knot.

As Lucinda carefully removed Faye's stained and patched cotton shift, she exposed an emaciated body covered in scars and sores—some scabbed over, some red and crusty. Her pelvic bones jutted from the sharp corners of her hips. Her belly was concave beneath the stark contrast of her ribcage. For a young woman of eighteen, her breasts were almost as flat as a ten-year-olds. Not a single ounce of fat was evident beneath her sallow skin.

I realized then I was only seeing the outer ravages to her young body. I could not even imagine the internal damage inflicted by the sexual assaults of her captors.

Nothing could prepare her parents for the sight of their daughter in such a fragile and horrific condition.

Lucinda helped Faye into the warm water and then wet the washcloth, lathering soap into it. With the softest of strokes, she caressed Faye's skin as if it were as delicate as rice paper, paying extra attention to the sores so she would not make them bleed.

For a little while, Faye watched the process until her eyelids grew heavy.

Lucinda folded a hand towel and placed it behind Faye's neck to cushion the hard edge of the bath tub.

Giving a sigh, Faye visibly relaxed, her thin form sinking deeper into the soothing warmth.

I didn't think I needed to remind Lucinda, but I did it anyway. "Be sure to put ointment on all the sores once Faye is bathed. Her father is a doctor and will bring stronger medicine to help her heal."

I was suddenly aware Lucinda was reading my thoughts. I sent back a message telepathically. *If you want to come with us, you can.*

She responded, *You don't know anything about me.*

I know all I need to know—that you have been a brave and loyal friend to Faye. I can see you care for her as if she was your sister. I'm sure she feels the same about you.

Faye helped me in Cancun.

How did she help you?

My mother died of cancer last year. I don't have any family there.

Where is your father?

I don't know. I never met him. Mama told me his name was Michael

Reed. She wrote to him at an address in Florida, telling him she was pregnant but she never heard from him again. After her death, a family I didn't know offered to let me live with them. I had nowhere else to go so I said yes. At first, everything was fine. But then the father and sons raped me. I ran away and went to the hotel where Mama had worked. They hired me to work in the play room where the guests leave their children while they go on excursions.

Where did you sleep?

In the play room. I would shower in a guest room after the guest checked out but before the maids cleaned the room. One night when I was sleeping, I was taken by a woman and a man to a house where there were other women and children. When I woke up, I didn't know how I got there and I was scared. That's where I met Faye.

Was it very far from the hotel in Cancun?

I don't think so.

Faye had dozed off. Lucinda stopped washing her and stared at the peaceful expression on her friend's face. She did not turn to look at me.

But I heard her unspoken question, *Do you know what they were going to do to Faye?*

I assumed she was to be sold to one of the owners of the clubs to become a prostitute.

No, she is too sick to earn them money. They were going to sell her for body parts.

At this horrible fact, I gasped.

As if she could have heard the telepathic conversation, Faye shook her head and started to cry. Suddenly, she began to thrash in the water, splashing Lucinda and the floor. Her eyes were still closed.

I assumed she was having a nightmare.

Lucinda kept reassuring Faye with kind words and a gentle touch that she was safe. Faye emerged from the blind panic, blinking and looking around, completely disoriented. The nightmares must have been a common occurrence because whatever Lucinda was saying and doing had the right affect. The two looked at one another, gazes locked.

I recognized they shared their own telepathic connection, understanding and supporting each other. I was in awe at Lucinda's maturity as well as her telepathy and wondered if she had other psychic gifts. She appeared to be a natural healer. Her focus and ability for her age was inspiring. "Lucinda, where did you learn how to communicate telepathically?"

"Mama. She said all of the women in her family had the same ability. I grew up thinking it was normal until I was old enough to realize it wasn't. Then I had to hide it so other kids would not tease me."

I smiled, nodding. "Me, too."

"After Mama died, she would visit me. Seeing her again was a blessing and a curse. I wasn't sure if I was losing my mind, so I shut down. I couldn't read anyone any more. I think that is why I was raped."

"No, Lucinda." I reached out a hand to her shoulder. "Don't think that. You are just as innocent as Faye. And just like I told her earlier, the situation wasn't your fault."

"But I should have known that man and his sons wanted to rape me. I should have—"

Faye reached out of the tub and wrapped her wet fingers around Lucinda's arm. With her other hand, she pressed a finger to her lips, then pointed at her ear, then pointed at me.

"Iiisss-ehn to 'er," Faye said, her words sounding as if her mouth was full of marbles. The enunciation was difficult but the hand signs spoke volumes. "Tehh 'er bow S-say-s-are."

"Okay, okay. Don't strain yourself." Lucinda looked at me. "She wants me to tell you about Caesar. When I noticed him at the river, I read his thoughts. It was the first time since Mama died. He asked us to go with him, and I knew he would help us. I said yes right away."

"I bet you were afraid."

"I was more afraid of what would happen if we stayed. I knew Faye did not have much time left before — well, we were to be separated."

You talk as if she does not know the plans for her, I said silently.

No, she does not know. I overheard it. I could not bear to tell Faye.

You are very young to carry such a burden.

I am very young for many things that have happened to me that should never happen to any girl or woman. Faye has had far worse. She does not need to know the men only valued her for body parts.

"We are the lucky ones, aren't we, Faye?" Lucinda had finished bathing her friend and helped her from the tub now filled with grayish water, drying her with soft pats of the towel.

I saw Lucinda yawn, and I stepped forward. "You are so tired. Please let me dress Faye so you can bathe."

She started to protest but Faye placed a finger on her lips again. "Iiisss oh-tay. Y-you tun."

"See? Even Faye agrees it is your turn."

Lucinda shrugged, and quickly doffed her shoes and shift and underpants without a moment's hesitation. Her skinny frame could use a few pounds but she looked downright robust compared to Faye.

A fact that made me suspect she hadn't been in captivity as long as Faye. I had just started to put ointment on Faye's sores when I spotted Lucinda raising a foot to step into the tub.

"Whoa. Hold on there. You don't have to bathe in dirty water."

"I don't mind."

"Nonsense. We have more than enough running water in this hotel than anyone could use. You will drain this tub and draw a fresh, hot bath."

"Yes, ma'am." She unplugged the tub and sat on the edge to wait for the water to drain.

With a last couple of dabs, I finished applying ointment. I was glad I had asked Alicia and José to buy gauze, bandages and peroxide. I opened the packages and used the materials to cover as many wounds as possible. Then, I slipped one of the clean nightgowns over Faye's head and upstretched arms.

"Now, we need to brush your hair." The wet blonde strands were a tangled mess, despite the cream rinse used on it in the tub. I started at the ends, trying not to pull too hard. "This may take a while."

Alicia walked in holding a milkshake in each hand with straws sticking out of the top. "Sandy came back with a special treat for you two. I hope you like chocolate."

CHAPTER 21

September 1, 1990
Saturday, 8:30 a.m.

Pete, Elegio, Carlos, Juan and Caesar had stopped by the hotel suite shortly after breakfast to see Faye and Lucinda. Each man received hugs of gratitude from both girls.

I sensed an undercurrent of seriousness from the men and directed Sandy to take the girls into the bedroom.

"What's going on?" I asked after the door was closed.

"We are returning to the compound," Pete said. "We don't have a plan yet, but we have talked to Ricardo about setting up surveillance from the abandoned barn overlooking the property while we figure out how to rescue the remaining children."

Juan waved a hand toward the closed door. "Now that we found the girls, Caesar and I have been released from this investigation. We are waiting for more agents from Mexico to join us here. Elegio and Carlos will only be temporary relief until the other men arrive."

Pete assured me he would come back to the hotel to play bodyguard for our group if any of us needed to go out. As long as we stayed inside as advised, we should be fine for a few hours without him.

"Promise me you won't try to get those kids out yet," I said. "From what I heard from Lucinda, I don't think any of them are in immediate danger."

"We have all agreed that anything we do right now could have grave ramifications on spiriting Faye and Lucinda out of the country. We will stand down until we get word they are in the air. Do you know how soon that might be?"

I shook my head. "We will know more after her parents arrive and her father has a chance to examine her. He's the doctor so he'll determine when she will be ready to travel."

«——»

Shortly after one o'clock in the afternoon, Faye was sleeping in the bedroom when we received word from José that the Franklin's private jet had landed. Lucinda remained close by the bedside, vigilant in her self-appointed duties as caretaker.

Through a conversation with Ricardo, I learned Dr. Robert Franklin was not only a highly regarded cardiac surgeon but also a volunteer physician for a global medical organization similar to Doctors Without Borders. Even though Mrs. Franklin had told me about their trips to Mexico City, she had failed to mention her husband flew to other countries, many in South America, to give his time and expertise at the local clinics in impoverished areas. Until their children were born, Mrs. Franklin had been a registered nurse in a trauma room and occasionally joined her husband on his humanitarian aid efforts.

Ricardo capitalized on the global reputation of Dr. Frank as an angel of mercy in third world countries, streamlining the procedure to bring the couple into Columbia at a last minute's notice. The bonus of a private jet owned by the charity organization was an additional god-send, offering an easier and safer means to sneak the girls out of the country before their captors could track them down and retrieve their human property.

The Franklins were traveling under the guise of bringing much-needed medical equipment to a local hospital in one of the poorest sections of the outlying neighborhoods. No matter what the circumstances with Faye, her father had to maintain the pretense of his visit to Cartagena and spend a reasonable amount of time with the patients and medical staff at the hospital to avoid the suspicions of government officials or the military.

The plane carried a full cargo of equipment and supplies that would legitimize Dr. Franklin's mission, as well as benefit many impoverished families. The situation was a win-win. That is, if the supplies reached their intended destination without being stolen by members of a drug cartel or common *banditos* to sell on the black market.

My mind was momentarily pulled back to the horrific assault on the young family from Sweden. There seemed to be no limit to the terror inflicted by the heartless criminals when stalking innocent victims, from children abducted for sweatshop labor to teens taken for the sex trade to adults brutalized for their valuables. And now, the latest information from Lucinda—killing to sell body parts. The thought of what might have happened to Faye sent a shudder down my spine.

"Deanne?" Sandy's voice startled me out of my dark rumination. "Sorry. I didn't mean to make you jump like that."

"I don't mind at all."

"I was wondering ... since Faye has such a hard time eating any food that isn't mashed up, maybe José and I could go to the market to buy jars of pureed baby food. We both thought the Franklins might be more comfortable with fewer people crowded into the room. And this is the middle of the day. And the market is only down the street."

"Slow down, Sandy." I held up my hands. "You've given me more than enough reasons to escape the confines of these four walls."

Frowning, she shook her head. "I'm not just making excuses to go outside. I really do think we should get some baby food. The jars will keep indefinitely, and we can heat them in a coffee cup of hot water from the coffee machine."

I grinned. "I know you aren't using Faye as an excuse. You're being very considerate, not only of Faye but of her parents."

Alicia joined us. "I like Sandy's idea of giving the family some privacy. I don't need to be here, either. I'll go with José and Sandy."

Fifteen minutes later, Dr. and Mrs. Franklin arrived at our room. They had been at the front desk when they recognized Alicia and José in the lobby. Had their initial meeting only been two weeks ago? Seemed more like two months to me. Probably felt like two years to the Faye's parents.

"Hello, Dr. Franklin." I shook his hand while drawing him into the room. The medical bag in his other hand seemed out of place with his cotton Hawaiian shirt and tan khaki shorts.

"Remember, it's just Robert." He gave me a smile that did not reach his eyes. I was sure he was relieved his daughter was safe but worry still etched his face.

I offered my hand to his wife who had moved out of the open doorway, allowing me to close the door. "I'm glad you both could get here so fast, Mrs. Franklin."

She pulled me into a tearful hug. "Oh, thank you, thank you, thank you for finding our Faye. I can never say it enough. And please call me Ida."

I returned the embrace. She smelled of flowery shampoo and expensive perfume. "You're welcome, but I only played a small part. A lot of people on our team were looking for her."

"I know. But you started the ball rolling. And you are here now when you could have left everything to Mr. Perez in Mexico City."

"Where is she?" Robert asked, his gaze scanning the room. "Can we see her?"

"She's resting comfortably in the adjoining bedroom. Before you go in, I would like to talk to you both. Please sit down." I waved a hand at the available seating.

The husband and wife sat on the sofa and took each other's hand. Her purse was on her lap. His black bag was on the floor at their feet.

I mentally braced myself for the news I had to deliver. "I know you are both medical professionals. But, more to the point, you are parents and I felt you need to be prepared for your daughter's appearance."

Robert started to rise to his feet. "We appreciate your

concern—"

With a hand placed on his arm, Ida pulled him back down. "Let her finish, Bobby. She wouldn't have asked to speak to us before seeing Faye if it wasn't important." She looked up at me. "Go ahead, Deanne."

I pulled a chair over to them and sat so I could be at their eye level.

"There are actually two things I want to let you know. First, Faye is extremely thin and appears to be suffering from a severe infection because she has sores all over her body. I am trying to prepare you for the initial shock."

"Again, we appreciate the warning but I am better suited to determine the state of her physical health."

"Bobby ..."

"I am, dear. This chit-chat is wasting my time."

I understood his impatience and didn't hold it against him. "Robert, your daughter has been sexually assaulted in every manner possible." Using a calm tone, I spoke slowly and carefully. "From what I have ascertained, she has been sodomized with foreign objects and raped—vaginally, anally and orally. Whatever infections she may have, at least one has swollen her tongue and throat to the point that she cannot talk."

Ida covered her face and sobbed. "Oh, dear God. No. NO! Noooo! My baby. My poor baby."

Robert put his arm around his wife, glaring hard while tears filled his eyes. "Why would you tell us such things? No, *how* could you know any of these things if Faye can't even talk? You're not a doctor. How could you know she was violated?

And with … objects?"

My telepathic connection with Faye had shown me everything she had seen with her own eyes, day after day, night after night. I saw the hands holding her wrists, her ankles. I saw the men on top of her, and the others waiting their turn. I saw the filthy fingers grip a broom handle, guiding it between her spread legs, heard the cackle of laughter, felt the stabbing pain deep inside. I felt the men behind her, bending her over a rail, a table, a bale of hay, tearing into her young body. When she screamed in pain, when she was no use to them in the usual way, she had her face pressed to their groins until she gagged and passed out.

Ida was still crying.

My heart went out to her. I hoped and prayed she would never know the specific details of abuse inflicted on her daughter.

"Robert, I had assumed you were aware I have psychic abilities. Your wife and I discussed it during our initial conversation."

"She said you had special abilities, yes. But I didn't realize you read minds!"

I felt his hostile skepticism but I did not let it ruffle me. I simply nodded. "I am telepathic."

I could not bear to tell him or Ida anything I witnessed in Faye's memories. They did not need to be subjected to nightmares of their daughter's torture. Although, I could tell them about Lucinda, who saw only some of the attacks. But she had heard so much more from her best friend before the swelling had silenced her.

"The second reason I wanted to talk to you is her friend, Lucinda, is in the other room with Faye. She is thirteen years old and has been taking care of your daughter as best she could. Lucinda was with Faye when our man, Caesar, helped them to escape. She has been through her own hell but nowhere near the extent Faye has endured. Still, she is vulnerable and afraid she will be separated from her best friend. She lost her mother last year and has no other family except for a father she has never met who was supposedly from Florida."

"Are you expecting us to take her with us?" Robert asked.

"I am not expecting anything other than your compassion when you meet her. Of course, your primary concern is your daughter, and I respect that. All I ask is that you do not dismiss Lucinda as if she doesn't exist. That little girl has been Faye's life line—and perhaps even the reason your daughter is still alive. I will make sure Lucinda is not abandoned or alone. But believe me when I say that is exactly how she will feel when you take Faye back to the states."

"Very well, then. We will keep your advice in mind." Robert reached down and picked up his medical bag. "Now, I would like to see Faye." He stood, helping Ida to her feet. "Will you be okay, dear?"

Taking a deep breath, she pulled back her shoulders and lifted her chin. Aside from some redness in her eyes, she appeared as if the distraught mother had vanished and the trained trauma nurse had just entered the room. No matter how she felt inside, she looked determined to be strong for her daughter.

At that moment, I was glad I had insisted on preparing them for what they would see in the next room. I rose from the chair and led the two to the door where I knocked twice quietly.

"Lucinda? Faye's parents are here to see her. Do you mind if we come in?"

A voice from inside the bedroom called out, "She's awake. Come in!"

As soon as her feet crossed the threshold, Ida dashed across the room to the bed, crying and carefully hugging her daughter who was crying just as hard.

Robert held back, watching the tearful reunion with his hand cupped over his mouth as if he could hide his raw emotions. He crossed his other arm at his waist as his body shook with sobs. Then he laughed nervously and continued crying. He was at a complete loss as to what to do with himself.

I moved closer and rested my palm on the small of his back, gently nudging him forward. "If you don't get in there, you'll never get your turn."

Nodding, he laughed again. "You're right." With long strides, He stepped up to the bed.

I saw Lucinda inching away from the other side and into the far corner. I gestured for her to come to me.

She gave me a sad, resigned look, dropped her chin to her chest, and shuffled silently across the beige carpet. As she passed the foot of the bed, she paused for a second, not looking at the joyful celebration. Her shoulders sagged an inch.

My chest felt tight with her heartbreak.

At the moment I felt her at my side, I put my arm around her slender shoulders and turned us both toward the door.

"Wait!" Ida said. "Don't go ... Lucinda, is it?"

Lucinda's chin jerked up. She glanced at me, a renewed sparkle in her eyes.

I winked at her, then tilted my head in the direction of the bed.

She smiled, then spun around. "Yes, it's Lucinda. Faye's best friend."

"Well, Lucinda-Faye's-Best-Friend," Ida teased. "I think Faye wants you to stick around."

Faye nodded, patting the mattress beside her.

Lucinda ran to the other side and launched herself into the air, careful to land a few inches away and not actually on her friend.

I left the four of them alone in the bedroom and went to make myself a cup of tea.

«—»

Forty minutes later, Sandy and Alicia returned from their shopping with José in tow. Each carried a grocery sack.

"Are they here yet?" Alicia asked, her gaze fixated on the closed door.

"Yes, they are all in the bedroom. I'm not sure how much longer they will be."

Sandy set her bag on the table. "How is Faye doing?"

"Better than yesterday, especially now that she's with her parents."

"How did they respond to the news about Lucinda?" José

asked, taking a red apple from his bag before he placed it on the table.

"Surprised. Robert isn't ready to commit to taking her back with them. But Faye will probably bend him before they leave."

The bedroom door creaked, turning our attention to the family slowly making their way into the room. Dr. Franklin and Mrs. Franklin helped their daughter walk to the couch and sit.

Lucinda seemed content to follow behind, but she soon claimed the cushion next to her best friend.

Faye appeared rested and relatively happy, despite the pain and other health issues, but her parents appeared emotionally and physically drained.

"Would you like some tea or coffee?" Alicia asked after introducing Sandy. "Have you had lunch? We are limited with food and beverages, but you are welcome to share whatever we have. Or we could order room service."

Ida Franklin smiled, shaking her head. "No, thank you. We don't want to impose more than we already are. We'll take Faye and Lucinda to our suite."

José cleared his throat, looking at me, his brows raised.

"Please reconsider moving the girls from here," I said, wishing to state the stipulations as gently as I could. "You and Mrs. Franklin are more high profile because you brought medical supplies. People may be curious about you. Plus you checked in as a married couple. Two unregistered guests in your suite would raise questions with the housekeeping staff. That they are young girls would also be a red flag. Illegal prostitution of minors to tourists is common. But a reputable doctor and his wife would not have girls in their room. Our suite is best because no one is paying attention to us."

"She's right, Bobby." Ida glanced between her husband and her daughter. "I think she'll be safer here. Besides, you'll be going back and forth to the clinic, leaving us alone most of the time."

Robert hesitated only a moment, struggling with his duty as a father to protect and care for Faye.

I was sure he had expected to swoop in and carry her off like the knight in shining armor that most dads want to be.

"All right. She stays. But she needs an I.V. hookup with glucose and stronger antibiotics that are in the extra luggage we brought along. We'll get the suitcases and bring them here. Once Faye is settled, Ida and I will grab a bite to eat and rest for a few hours. I need to report to the hospital before the day is over. But she can come back to take care of our daughter."

"Sounds good to me," I said, pleased at his decision.

CHAPTER 22

Two hours later, the Franklins had come and gone, leaving Faye on the couch with the I.V. drip. Her father wanted her to stay in the bedroom, but she couldn't bear to be shut off from the rest of us, even if Lucinda stayed with her. I suspected she was considering Lucinda more than herself. She didn't want her young friend to be isolated in the bedroom without someone who could actually talk to her.

Sandy taught Lucinda to play gin rummy, and Alicia read a paperback novel by Tess Gerritsen that she'd bought in the hotel gift shop. José was in his room next door, on call if we needed anything.

Pete had returned from surveillance on the compound, impressed by the four younger agents who would be taking turns on their watch. He assured me nothing would happen until a plan was firmly in place. But he expressed added concern about the dangerous location in the middle of rival cartels. Satisfied all was well in our suite, he went to his own room down the hall.

Now was a good time to check in with my family. Using my portable phone in the bedroom, I talked with Kitty for about fifteen minutes, learning Ryan had found Nadine a job in a small construction office owned by a friend. Lisa was giving Nadine the first three months rent-free at the apartment she owned with her brother, Tommy. This would give Nadine a chance to get on her feet. I asked how Nadine was doing with her pregnancy. Apparently, all was well. Then, of course, I inquired about my shepherd, Heidi. I was sure she missed me as much as I missed her.

After talking with Kitty, I called Ryan. I missed him, too. A lot. I was happy to hear he missed me, too. I liked how he asked about my kids and my dog. I thanked him for helping Nadine. He related so well with people and was great with animals— my type of person.

He listened with rapt attention as I shared the details of Faye's capture and her parents' arrival, explaining the cover story for their trip to Cartagena.

"Her father told me Faye is suffering from Gonorrhea, which is also in her mouth. She has a serious ear and throat infection, and she cannot fly until the swelling goes down because of the danger of rupturing an eardrum."

"So, you're staying longer?"

"I have to, Ryan. Please don't be too upset."

"Honey, I am not the least bit upset. Disappointed, maybe. But I know you well enough now to know you see things through to the end. I wouldn't expect you to leave Faye or Lucinda right now. Especially that thirteen-year-old orphan. Christ, what a bad lot she drew. Somebody ought to find her daddy in Florida and kick him in the ass for abandoning his kid before she's even born."

I chuckled at his righteous indignation. "That's the guy I know and love."

"Hell, I'd find him myself and castrate the bastard."

He was on a roll, which only made me laugh. "No, you wouldn't!"

"Why wouldn't I?"

"Because you would land in some Southern prison for murder and I would only get conjugal rights every month or two. Do you know how expensive flying from California would be?"

His bark of laughter was so loud I yanked the receiver from my ear. "Oh, Sugar, I don't know what I did to deserve you. Keep up this sweet-talking and I might have to fly down to Columbia and book a honeymoon suite in that hotel. As soon as we get your clients on their plane, I take you to bed for a month of Sundays."

"Wow, that sounds too good to be true. Be careful, I just might take you up on that offer."

"Short of surprising you in the hallway tomorrow, I'll start making plans for a real vacation for us as soon as you get home."

"Just remember I'll need a few days to catch up at my office before I can fly off somewhere again."

"You got it, honey." He paused.

I sensed he had something else to say. "What is it?"

"Well ... If you come home with a thirteen-year-old orphan and tell me you want to adopt her, I might need some time to wrap my head around the idea, but it wouldn't send me running the other direction. I love you, Deanne. Do whatever you need to do, and I'll support you one hundred percent."

For a long moment, I was silent, trying to form words around the enormous lump in my throat. Finally, I managed to whisper, "Mister Ryan Gibb, you are the most amazing human being on the planet. I couldn't love you more than I love you right now. If I wasn't such an old fashioned girl, I would ask you to marry me."

"Old-fashioned? Ha! You are the most liberal-minded female I have met!"

"I take that as a compliment."

"It is! Besides, you wouldn't dare deprive me of the chance to get down on bended knee with a little black velvet box in my hand. Why, it would break my heart."

"Well, we can't have that, can we?" I was enjoying our funny, loving banter so much that I hated to get off the phone. But the time had come to say good-bye, which we did in our usual back-and-forth way.

When I hung up, I felt like I was floating on air. I was crazy in love, and I didn't care how silly or sappy anyone might think I was. I fell backward on the bed and wrapped my arms around myself, wishing Ryan was holding me tight. Too bad I left my ruby slippers at home.

«—»

A few minutes later, I returned to the living room area. Faye, Sandy and Lucinda were in the same places I had left them.

Alicia closed the book with a snap. "Another bites the dust," she said with satisfaction.

"You read that one in record time."

"The plot was that good. Gerritsen is one of my favorite authors. I start reading and can't put it down."

I agreed with a nod. "Faye, can I get you anything?" She shook her head but I actually saw a slight smile on her face.

"You're looking better already." I turned back to Alicia. "I need a haircut. Could I talk you into giving me just a little trim?"

She hopped up. "I'd love to! I've read everything I brought with me already, and I'm bored."

"I know."

"Sorry, I am not complaining."

"I can tell. I sense you are frustrated, though."

"A little. I want to help free those children. I get the feeling the guys won't invite me to join them because I am a woman."

"Tell José to inform Ricardo you want to be included."

She tilted her head. "Do you think that will make a difference?"

"You won't know if you don't ask."

"Will you mind if I leave and work with them?"

"Of course not. I think you joining the team would be a great idea. The children have been abused by men and would feel safer with a woman. I'll drop a bug in Ricardo's ear the next time I talk to him. Two cheerleaders are better than one."

Alicia gave me a big hug. "Thanks. I've been thinking about this all day."

"I knew you were having a debate within yourself about something."

"I didn't want you to think I was running out on you, José and Sandy."

"Faye's parents are here now. I think everything is under control. José said we could call the team if we needed help."

"Then I've made my decision. I am going next door and talk to him."

Fifteen minutes later, José came over and asked me to join them. Ricardo had asked to talk to me. Now was my chance to convince him Alicia would be an asset in the effort to rescue the kids at the compound.

After we exchanged greetings, Ricardo was more interested in what I felt about the team freeing the children than in Alicia joining them. I understood he wanted my gut feelings, any forewarning. I had not experienced any sort of precognition about the kids, which I told him.

"I would need to go there to see if I pick up on anything," I explained. "Being in closer proximity to the camp doesn't guarantee I will perceive anything helpful, but I am willing to try."

"Then go out to the stakeout on the barn and take Alicia. José. too. Have him rent a non-descript car to transport you. Don't be gone too long. I will let Pete know to keep an eye on your room."

"I will call Mrs. Franklin. She and her husband are resting in their room after their long trip, but I'm sure she would be glad to sit with her daughter."

"Oh, and Deanne? I'm sure Pete has already warned you about the danger. Traveling through that area is bad enough for a man. Even with José as your driver, you should not let anyone see you."

"As a woman, you mean." I caught and held Alicia's gaze.

"Yes, that's right."

"Alicia has her magic suitcase of disguises. She and I will

dress up as men. Problem solved."

There was a moment of silence on the other end of the line, then a chuckle. "Very good. Alicia will be a good asset after all."

After I promised to report back at the end of our short trip, I let Ida know she was needed in the suite, which pleased her enormously. Robert would take the opportunity to go to the hospital. The pilot of the private plane and a medical technician trained to set up the new equipment initially remained behind at the airport to be present during the inspection of the cargo by a military troop. Once cleared, everything would be transported in a large truck.

Robert was expected to meet the pilot and technician to supervise unloading and placement of the larger pieces. He would be away for several hours, possibly after dark, which didn't set well with me. Sometimes doctors thought they were immune to attacks. I hoped Robert Franklin was not one of them. I informed Alicia she and I were going to the abandoned barn, but only for a few hours.

"I understand why Ricardo wants you to go, but why me? Is he putting me on the team?"

"I don't know but he did ask you to dress us as men for our travel. Maybe he will make his decision based on how things go today."

"Great! I'm willing to give it my best shot."

Her suitcase of make-up and disguises was stored on a high shelf in the closet by the door. She retrieved it and lugged it into the bedroom where we could try on different clothes.

She put on a wig and heavy mustache. Her appearance

immediately changed. "What do you think?"

"I think this could be fun."

"We can wear Levi's, a shirt with a jacket to cover our chests and, with a wig and mustache. Nobody will know we are women. The hardest thing to remember is to walk like a man."

"We'll have to practice." I walked into the living room area to check my appearance with Sandy, Lucinda and Faye. "What do you think?"

They looked up and gasped.

I could see from the wide-eyed looks on their faces, that the disguises were good.

"Wow, you don't look like yourself," Sandy said, jumping off the portable bed. "Can I go with you?"

"I'm afraid not. You're a bit too well-endowed to convince anyone you are a man."

Lucinda snickered. "Unless you smoosh down your boobies with tape. No, that would not work. You would go *POP* right in someone's face."

Sandy's mouth dropped open.

Faye made funny snorting noises with her nose, the best she could do in lieu of a real laugh.

Lucinda rose to her feet while still on the portable bed, stepping on playing cards as she stuffed a sofa pillow under her Princess top, expanding her chest to monstrous proportions. "I have big boobies like you. Now I am so pretty. Pretty as a real princess!" She put one hand on a hip and sashayed in a circle while balancing on the flimsy mattress.

Faye snorted hardier.

Sandy swatted playfully at Lucinda's leg. "Give me that

pillow!" she demanded with no serious threat in her voice.

Lucinda pinched the fabric over her phony breasts and stretched the t-shirt out more. "They're getting bigger!"

By now, Alicia had emerged from the bedroom to see what all the commotion was about. She laughed harder than anyone.

With a sweep of her arm, Sandy caught the back of Lucinda's knees, buckling them. Lucinda went down on the mattress and Sandy practically fell on her, yanking the pillow out from under the shirt. Holding the pillow up high in victory, she rested her other palm on Lucinda's flat chest. "Okay, little sister, say 'Uncle' or you're going to eat your boobies."

Lucinda laughed harder. "No, I won't say it."

They went back and forth until Sandy shrugged, "Okay, you asked for it. Time to *eat* the *boobies!*" She dropped the pillow onto Lucinda's face and wriggled it back and forth.

In an instant, the peals of laughter from the thirteen-year-old turned to shrieks of fright. Thrashing her arms and legs, she fought against the terror of suffocation.

Sandy immediately yanked away the pillow but Lucinda was in the full throes of a panic attack. Sandy shushed her, trying to calm her and stop the screams. Alicia rushed to Faye, stopping her from pulling out the I.V. in an attempt to reach her little friend. I moved toward Lucinda, realizing too late my disguise was not helping. She had mistaken me for one of the captors.

A loud pounding on the door finally stop the chaos.

"FAYE! DEANNE!" The person was Ida Franklin.

I dashed to the door and let her in.

She took one look at me and jumped back. "Don't you touch me! Who are you? Where's my daughter?"

I raised my hands. "It's me, Deanne! I'm in disguise. Everything is okay. No one is hurt. Faye is fine. Sandy and Lucinda were horsing around, and the action got out of hand."

"Horseplay?" Ida huffed, confusion changing to anger. "You call screaming bloody murder at the top of her lungs *horseplay?*"

Sandy was suddenly at my side. "I'm very sorry, Mrs. Franklin. We were teasing each other and joking and even got Faye laughing for a bit. But when I tried to make Lucinda eat her boobies—uh, I mean, *pillow*, I never expected her to freak out."

I put my arm around Sandy and looked at Ida. "The mistake was an innocent one. The girls really were having fun. And I think, for a few minutes, they took Faye's mind off her pain. Sandy has no knowledge of what Lucinda has been through. The playful act of the pillow in the face triggered a memory. Lucinda was reacting to something else that had been done to her."

I felt Lucinda's presence behind me, hiding as if she could make herself disappear. I reached around, took her hand and gently drew her around to my other side. I lifted her chin with the crook of my finger. "Everything's okay, Lucinda. You aren't in trouble. No one is mad at you."

Her lower lip trembled. She dropped her gaze to her bare feet. "The dad ... and his sons ... they put a pillow over my face so no one else in the house would hear me when they raped me."

"I didn't know." Sandy raced around me and grabbed Lucinda, hugging her tight. "I'm so sorry. I didn't know."

CHAPTER 23

"Let's go, ladies," José said when he returned from renting a car. Glancing at our attire, he added, "Or I should say *gentlemen*. I have bags of groceries in the trunk, replacement supplies for the guys at the barn. Ricardo's orders. I also have bottles of water in the car and some fruit for us."

As the three of us walked through the lobby, I was relieved to see so few people mingling about. I felt weird in my disguise.

"Relax," Alicia muttered behind her black mustache. "If anyone is thinking about us at all, they'll just think we're just some skinny men."

"Who are you calling skinny?" José pretended to look offended, folding his arms over his chest.

She chuckled.

"You are thoroughly enjoying yourself, aren't you?" I was clearly not as comfortable in the disguise as Alicia

"Yeah, actually. I've done this several times. It's fun."

"Okay, I'll work on it."

At the car, José gestured to Alicia opening the front passenger door. "I think you should sit in the back seat with Deanne. It is lower and harder for anyone to see you."

Suddenly, Pete appeared out of nowhere and stepped around Alicia.

She jerked back her hand. "What the—?"

"Get in," he ordered, opening the door and sliding in the seat Alicia had been expecting to occupy.

We scrambled inside, me behind José in the driver's seat and Alicia behind Pete.

"I thought Ricardo wanted you to stay behind to watch the room." I rested a hand on the back of the front seat.

Pete shrugged. "No offence to José, but the girls are safer in the hotel suite than you three will be in a few minutes. He wants me to get you back safe and sound."

As we drove out of the city, he filled us in on a few other little details about the compound located about four hundred kilometers from the main roads. Security appeared to be limited. Juan and Caesar had already set up video cameras on a tractor at the rear of the property, taping images of two different men, although a total of four were present.

To avoid suspicion, our guys made sure to act like farmers. They were all the approximate same size and wore similar clothes. They worked twelve-hour surveillance shifts, allowing themselves to be seen doing farm chores out in the open.

«—»

Forty five minutes later, we pulled up in front of a dilapidated gray barn. We each grabbed a bag of food and walked inside. Hammocks hung limp in the corners. Wooden crates for seats were set on their ends around a make-shift table of saw-horses and a splintery door broken off the front of a stall.

A single stubby candle sat in the middle of a battered pie

tin. Now I understood why we'd brought a box of candles.

Carlos and Elegio climbed down a loft ladder and greeted Pete and José like long-lost comrades. Having their fun, they ignored Alicia and me entirely, pretending we were strangers. Strange *men*, that is. When the joke was over, we got down to the reason we were there.

"So, Alicia, we heard you want to join us," Elegio said. "You can take my place. I would love to go home."

Alicia shook her head. "I had no intention of replacing anyone. I only want to help. Pete said you have taken some videos. Can we see them?"

Carlos spoke. "Sure, but they don't have much. From time to time, you can see children playing soccer outside the compound in the empty field."

"Have any children been taken away?"

"No. But five or six children arrived by truck day before yesterday."

"I'm just trying to get a feel for how many might be in there."

"We estimate between twenty and thirty. Hard to know the ages because they are too far away for us to see clearly."

I was allowing Alicia to do all the talking so she could get a better idea of whether she could work with this team. But I had work to do, too. "Is there a place where I can observe the compound?"

"The loft," answered Carlos. "That's where we were when you arrived. There is a great view. I'll show you."

I followed him up the narrow ladder to the barn loft, the strap of my large bag slung over my neck and across my body, allowing my hands to be free to grab the rails. My binoculars in my bag made it thump heavily against my hip each time I raised my foot to the next rung.

A dirty bench seat from an old car had been braced against a post to keep it upright. Set slightly to one side, the seat could not be easily seen through the opening where hay was usually hoisted into the loft. The view of the compound was perfect.

"Thanks, Carlos. I hope you don't mind, but I would like to spend some time alone up here."

"*No problemo.*"

I waited as he descended the ladder, then I sat down and settled back, almost grateful to have a broken spring digging into the small of my back to keep me awake and alert. Within moments, I saw the gate open and about ten children walk to the field next door. I took out my binoculars and watched. Two children followed behind carrying a ball. All the children appeared to be healthy.

I stood and went to the edge of the loft to call for Alicia to come up.

She climbed the ladder quickly and easily.

I assumed she wanted to demonstrate her agility to the men, in case they were observing her to report to Ricardo.

"I thought you wanted to be alone," she said without the faintest sound of heavy breathing from the climb.

"I do, but children just came out of the compound and I wanted you to see."

"Thanks. By the way, I am not so sure I want to join the team out here. This primitive set up has made me appreciate our hotel."

"You don't like living in a rustic, open-air hotel?"

"Not so much." Her mouth twisted into a grimace as she gestured to the crummy seat. "I don't want to sound like a spoiled priss. I could handle the dirt and spider webs. I'm just not so sure I could handle a confrontation out here in the middle of cartel lands. Not even Ricardo is comfortable sending us out here with José. He had to pull Pete off guard duty to protect our asses. As soon as I stepped out of the car, I felt a shiver down my spine. I just don't think I am cut out for this case."

"Is that what your gut is telling you?"

"Yeah, good old woman's intuition."

"Then listen to it."

With a nod, Alicia borrowed my binoculars and after several minutes gave them back. "These kids appear very normal. What do you think?"

"I think they don't know what is in their future."

An elderly woman and man opened the gate and said something to the children that we couldn't hear because of the distance. The adults returned to the compound, leaving the children to continue playing soccer.

"I think the children we are seeing are all young boys." I again surveyed the group.

Alicia took back the binoculars to check. "How can you tell?"

"They play like boys, not girls."

"That means they kidnap both sexes?"

"Appears so." I accepted the return of the binoculars. "Okay, that's all I wanted you to see. Can you give me a few minutes alone?"

"Sure."

After I watched her disappear back down the ladder, I could hear her whispering to the team about what we had seen.

I sat with my binoculars, watching the children for about thirty minutes until another man called to them. They immediately stopped playing soccer and returned to the interior of the compound.

I needed to expand my energy and allow myself to feel the children's energy. It took me longer than usual to get to a meditative state. I had to make a conscious effort to ignore my own wayward thoughts and to follow the energy.

Later, we could analyze my perception with what the team already knew.

Soon, I started to sense information coming to me, settling into my mind as if it were knowledge I had already acquired and not something new. I like to think of the process like having a memory of an event without actually experiencing the event.

After my energy returned to where I was sitting, I knew both boys and girls were in the compound. I knew they were citizens of different countries. I also knew as sure as I was sitting in the loft that many children would be hurt if the team went charging into the compound with guns firing. From what I observed, even though the children were locked inside at night, they had freedom during the day. They were fed and bathed regularly, which was a better life than what they'd had for some of them. I wished I could talk with each child individually, but that was impossible.

I returned to the team below. They knew why I was there, that I had unexplainable skills. They were waiting for my assessment. I was grateful for their respect, instead of ridicule.

"I don't care how many people you bring here to rescue the children, a plan to invade the camp won't work. The children are expendable to their captors. If the compound is raided, I believe they will not risk capture by taking time to load the kids on a vehicle to escape. And they wouldn't leave any alive to identify them."

Pete spoke. "Any sound of gunfire will bring the fires of hell raining down from all of the drug cartels that make this area their home. If the kids are massacred by their caretakers, they'd likely die in cross-fire from the rival gangs. Our own team wouldn't make it out either."

Carlos rubbed the back of his neck with his palm. "We have got to come up with a plan. I don't want to leave these kids here."

"None of us do," I said. "It's time for us to get back to the hotel."

Once in the car, I fell back in my seat, feeling drained. The countryside was beautiful. We passed through jungles that I would have loved to explore, but at least five drug cartels had a presence here. They were fighting each other for the drug routes. We couldn't trust law enforcement. If the drug cartel requested the services of law enforcement, refusal was not an option. If officers don't accept, they risked having their family executed for lack of cooperation.

I turned to look at Alicia. "Any ideas?"

"I don't know. I feel frustrated there are so many children."

"What do you think about buying the children?" I asked, the thought coming out of my mouth as quickly as it popped into my head.

José spoke up from the driver's seat. "How would that work?"

"If someone offered to purchase children to work in a factory, he could ask how much is paid for each child. He might even learn about their health."

"Don't you think they would check out the factory?" Alicia asked.

"I expect they would. We would have to get a factory owner to agree to be part of our ploy."

"Do you have anyone in mind?"

"Yes, I do. But I don't have his phone number. I can call Kitty tomorrow for it. But I think we need more than just one person to be interested in buying children."

"We know the children are used as slave labor or prostitution," José added. "We wouldn't want the kidnappers to think they need a larger supply of children because of a new demand."

"Excellent point, José," I said, leaning forward to pat his shoulder. "You are learning quickly. I think you will make a great investigator, if that is what you decide to do."

He was quiet a moment. "I'm grateful for your vote of confidence, Deanne. After being on this case with all of you, I am not certain I have the stomach for the violence and torture, especially against the children."

Pete suddenly broke his silence. "If we don't help them, who will?"

FINDING FAYE • 215

The rest of us nodded.

"Don't beat yourself up, kid. If you aren't cut out for this line of business, you have nothing to be ashamed about. It's not for everyone."

《——》

On our return to the hotel, once again I felt as if everyone in the lobby stared. I could hardly wait to take off the wig and mustache.

Entering our suite, we found Faye sitting up at the table with her mother and Lucinda.

"Faye!" Alicia said, "You look like you're feeling better."

"Ye-s, Th-ank 'ou." The words were not very clear, but so much better than before.

Ida had been reading aloud from the book, *Black Beauty*. "This is one of Faye's favorite stories. Lucinda seems to be enjoying the story, but I don't know how much she understands."

Lucinda smiled. "I understand it."

Sandy came out from the bedroom. "How did it go?"

"Fine." Alicia pulled off her fake mustache, wincing. "Ouch. Next time, I need less spirit gum to attach it."

"Well?" Sandy stood with her arms out to her side. "Come on, tell me everything."

"There isn't much to tell," I reassured her as I pulled off my mustache. "We went out there to get a look at the compound. Ricardo wanted me to get a feel for it, find out if I received any sort of psychic message or premonition."

"Did you?"

"I told the others that a raid was a poor idea. Too much risk to the lives of the children. But we may have thought of another way."

I explained the conversation in the car about a ploy to buy the kids. There was still a lot to work out. No plan is foolproof, but this one had to be as close to perfect to save as many lives as possible.

"I can't talk anymore," I said, scratching my wig in an attempt to soothe my itchy scalp. The whole thing moved back and forth.

Lucinda wrinkled her nose. "Ewww, don't do that. It looks creepy."

I grinned. "Yes, I know. And it feels creepy. Now if you will excuse me while I go into the bedroom to get out of this get-up."

Lucinda giggled. "Get *out* of the get *up?*"

She was still giggling as I left the room. Alicia followed and Ida went back to reading *Black Beauty*.

After showering and washing my hair, I dressed and called Kitty to say hello but also to ask her for the number of the clothing factory owner. Afterward, I called him and left a message, then called Ryan. I was getting homesick. No, I was already homesick. Faye was responding to the antibiotics, for which I was really glad. Now, all I could think about was going home. I missed my daughter, my son, my lover, my life.

José brought us all dinner from a great seafood restaurant.

"José, you are the best sidekick ever."

He blushed.

Sandy leaned on him, her hands wrapped around his arm.

"He's more than a sidekick, Deanne. He's an all-around awesome guy, guide, teacher, driver, you-name-it."

Ducking his head, he blushed a deeper pink, if that was possible.

The two of them had clearly become close friends. I wouldn't be surprised if they stayed in touch after we finished the assignment.

CHAPTER 24

September 2, 1990
Sunday, 8:30 a.m.

The entire team that had originally been formed to find Faye agreed to meet in José's hotel room to discuss the rescue of the children at the compound. Even Juan and Caesar drove into town, temporarily leaving the barn unattended. The energy was exciting with a "Wild West" enthusiasm from some of the guys.

Everyone was talking fast in Spanish, their primary language, unlike Alicia, Sandy and me. Sandy was completely lost. I could follow most of the conversation, even though they talked over each other's words and used slang. Despite learning Spanish when I was eleven years old, I had to stop the conversation a couple times for clarification. After a few of my interruptions that slowed the discussion, I decided to rely on José to fill me in later on anything I might have missed.

I raised my hand instead of my voice. The noise in the room suddenly vanished. Like school boys taught to respect the teacher, the team looked at me expectantly.

"It sounds like you all have some strong opinions about a rescue operation. I would like to suggest bringing Lucinda here. She was inside and knows a lot about the caretakers and the kids. She could give us valuable insight."

"Go get her." Caesar gestured toward the door.

I could imagine this group bombarding the girl with questions from every angle with the same loud volume created by everyone talking at once. This time, I held up both hands. "Wait a minute! You need to remember she is only thirteen years old. She has a lot of courage for a person of her age, but she is easily intimidated. She needs to be nurtured and heard."

I sensed several of the men's bafflement. I doubt any had been trained in their respective military or law enforcement backgrounds to nurture anyone to get the answers they wanted. Not that any would stoop to water-boarding, but gentle persuasion was hardly an interrogation tactic.

I watched everyone glance around and give an approving nod. José left the room and returned a few minutes later with Lucinda.

"Who is with Faye?" I asked, "Other than her mother?"

"No one," answered Lucinda. "Dr. Franklin went to the hospital."

I hadn't realized the meeting would leave our clients unattended. Dropping the ball was not like me. "Sandy, I want you to go next door and stay with them. We'll let you know what is going on."

Sandy looked chagrined. She quickly left the room. Alicia gave me a puzzled look. "I'll explain later."

Carlos took charge of asking questions. He offered her a seat. "Lucinda, would you like something to drink?"

"No, thank you."

I watched the men soften as she repeated the story of her

mother's death, the family who took her in and ultimately betrayed her when the father and his sons used her for their own pleasure. Hearing the details brought tears to my eyes all over again. She reached the part about her abduction from the play room at the hotel.

"Were you hurt by the kidnappers?" Carlos asked.

She gave him a puzzled expression.

I sensed she did not know how to answer. There are many ways to be hurt.

Carlos clarified, "Were you hit or pushed or slapped?"

She nodded. "Two or three times, I was pushed to the ground. One time I was punched in the back."

"What about sexually?" I asked.

For a brief moment, I felt as everyone else was holding their breath at the same time. The topic was a tricky path with a young girl. None of the men wanted to appear as though they were titillated by her sexual abuse.

Lucinda cocked her head to one side, considering her response. "Yes, I was forced to sleep with men, to do many things to them and let them do things to me. Sometimes, they took movies of me. The big man told me I would be famous one day. I told the big man I didn't want to do sex anymore. The big man asked me if I wanted to work hard in the fields under a hot sun. I said I wasn't crazy, but I wasn't lazy either. I could cook or sew. The next thing I knew, I was on a little boat with other girls.

"The trip was scary. The sea was rough and the boat was small. One girl kept throwing up. One of the men threatened to throw her overboard if she didn't stop. On the third day, she was still sick so he threw her into the ocean." She shuddered and took a deep breath. "I can still hear her screams. She was only ten years old."

Elegio and Juan surreptitiously turned their faces away and moved back against the wall, hiding their raw emotions over a little girl discarded like trash in the ocean, left alone to drown. Caesar remained stoic, his jaw clenched. Pete's eyes narrowed.

Carlos cleared his throat, as did a few others, again masking their sadness. "Did they feed you at the compound?"

"Yes, in the morning and night."

"How did you and Faye escape?"

"We were told to find a plant by the river that would help Faye's infection. She was awful sick. Someone watched us for a long time from the look-out. Faye kept sitting down to rest in the tall grass and reeds along the bank. I would beg her to stand so the guard did not come looking for us. The last time I checked, the man was not watching us anymore. Then we heard a whistle. I turned toward the sound, and I saw that man." She pointed at Caesar. "He called Faye by name and told her he was sent by her parents to take her home. At first, we didn't believe him, but Faye couldn't ask him questions because she couldn't talk. So I did." She gave a feeble smile. "I knew if we didn't go with him, something bad was going to happen to Faye."

Carlos frowned. "Do you mean he threatened you so you would go with him?"

"No! He was nice to us."

She started swinging her feet back and forth. Her fingers wrapped around the seat of the chair.

I projected my thoughts to Lucinda, *Tell them what was going to happen to Faye. She's not here. She won't find out.*

Lucinda jerked her head around until her gaze landed on me a few feet away. *What if they tell her parents?*

I tipped my head toward Carlos. *Ask him not to tell. Ask them all to keep it a secret from Faye.*

Lucinda turned her attention back to Carlos, but not before she scanned the room to meet the gaze of everyone there. "Faye can never know what I am about to tell you. You can't say anything to her or to her mother and father. Do I have your promise? All of you?"

Carlos and the others murmured their agreement.

"Faye was going to be sold for body parts. That was the only way to make money off of her because she was so ugly with sores and infections."

Caesar added, speaking to the entire room. "The black market for body parts is very, very lucrative. Rich *Americanos* and Europeans will pay tens of thousands of their dollars for one organ, more if it is for their child. Children's organs are smaller, and not easy to find. They bring a premium price. A parent will pay whatever is necessary. Faye is only eighteen. Even if she was capable of working in the clubs, she could never earn the million or more that would be paid for her skin, her bones, her heart." He shook his head. "I'm sorry to say she is worth more to them dead than alive. Much, much more."

"But she is sick," Alicia said. "Venereal disease would kill an organ recipient, wouldn't it?"

He shrugged. "Do you think these people care what happens to a sick *Gringo* kid? No. Not just the sick ones like

Faye are picked. This is another reason why I asked for this assignment to rescue the children."

I watched Lucinda listening to Caesar. Her face grew pale as she realized she and all the other children were vulnerable to the same fate. The information replayed in her thoughts, over and over—

Children's organs are smaller, not easy to find.

Lucinda, stop! My silent plea reached through her fear before it escalated. *Don't think about this right now. Clear your mind, or you will not be able to focus on the questions. You must focus, Lucinda. To help them rescue the children.*

She did not look at me but gave a single nod. *I will.*

Carlos brought us back to the interview. "Lucinda, how did you find out about their plans for Faye?"

"I overheard them talking when I came to the kitchen for water. I always got food and water for Faye because no one else would go near her. They were all scared she would give her infections to them so they stopped raping her and left her alone. I was afraid for her. But I couldn't tell her why. Nobody should ever hear that they were no good for anything but being cut up to have your parts put in other people just so they can live."

For the first time, Lucinda crumpled into tears. "I-I didn't want to lose her. She is my best friend. She is my big sister."

I stepped forward. "Maybe we can take a break. Give Lucinda a chance to compose herself."

"No," Lucinda said, bringing up her head. "I want to stay. I want to help. Ask me questions. As many as you want. I will stay in this chair all day and night if it will help you save the other children."

"Very well," Carlos said. "How many grown up people are working at the compound?"

"Four. Three men and one woman."

"That's it?"

"I only saw four."

"Who did the cooking?"

"The children. If we didn't do chores, we didn't eat."

"Did you see any guns?"

"Yes, one of the men had a gun. I saw a gun under his shirt."

"Did you know any of the children?"

"No."

"Do you know what country they are from?"

"Mexico, I guess. All but one spoke Spanish like me. Faye talked with the other girl, but I couldn't understand them. She said it was something called 'French'."

After three hours, I insisted on a break for the whole group. Alicia, Lucinda and I returned to our suite. Faye was asleep in the bedroom. Her mother dozed in an easy chair near her daughter, a romance novel splayed open on her lap.

Lucinda kept yawning repeatedly so I coaxed her to lay down on the other side of Faye for a short nap. I knew the Q-and-A had been emotionally exhausting. I closed the bedroom door behind me as I left.

CHAPTER 25

Our break lasted an hour and a half, because I would not wake Lucinda from her nap. I used the time to again call the owner of the clothing factory in Los Angeles. I was thrilled to make the connection and explain the situation about the children. I was even more excited to have some news to share with the rest of the team when we reconvened.

Lucinda awoke blurry-eyed but willing and eager to return to José's room and face more questions.

"Before you start," I said to Carlos, as I glanced around the gathered group, "I reached the factory owner a little while ago. He said he would help but he didn't want his name used. We could, however, use the name of his company. He also offered to talk with his colleagues in the garment district to find anyone else willing to help us. One of our team will have to pose as the owner to negotiate a deal for the children."

"That might work," Elegio said.

Carlos withdrew a notepad from his back pocket and flipped it open. "We have made a list of more questions. Are you ready, Lucinda?"

"Yes."

"Do you know the names of any of your kidnappers?"

"The woman was Maria. One of the men was called Papo. The man who brought food to us was Mario."

"Did you hear them use any last names?"

"No. They didn't talk much except to tell us what they wanted us to do."

"What about the men on the boat that brought you to Columbia?"

"The mean man who threw the girl off the boat was Eric Morales."

"How do you know that?"

"His passport fell out of his pocket and landed by my foot. It fell open and I saw his name inside. The other man got real mad and called Eric all kinds of bad names."

"What did Eric do?"

"Nothing. He said all of us children were too stupid to know how to read or know what a passport was. The man told Eric he was stupid."

"What about the other man on the boat? Did you get his name?"

"Only a first name of Mateo."

"Can you describe these men?"

"Yes. I will never forget what they looked like."

"Do you think you would you recognize a photo of them?"

"Yes."

Carlos signaled to Elegio who stepped forward with a folder, opening it and handing pictures to the young girl. "These are men who work at the dock. Do you recognize any of them?"

I watched Lucinda carefully scrutinizing each photograph, then shake her head as she moved to the next one.

She passed them back to Elegio. "They were younger than

these men. Also, Mateo had a scar on the left side of his face and his left arm."

"How big was the scar?"

Her fingers traced a circle from her cheek to her temple. "The skin was lighter and shiny smooth. His left eye looked crooked, too. He had the same kind of scars on his arm and hand."

Alicia offered, "Sounds like a scar from being burned."

Lucinda shrugged. "I don't know, but he didn't like anyone to look at him. I think that is why he didn't care when Eric threw the girl off the boat. She was always looking at him."

"I thought Eric threw her overboard because she kept throwing up."

"That was what he said but she only really threw up twice. The rest of the time was just gagging. We didn't have anything to eat so she did not have anything in her stomach to throw up."

"I thought they fed you in the morning and at night."

"At the compound. Not when on the boat. We had nothing to eat or drink except water."

Lucinda held up her hand and made the symbol of a zero with her fingers. I really liked this girl and wondered if I could adopt her. Ryan's comment popped into my mind and I smiled to myself.

"Lucinda, you are a smart young lady. Do you have some ideas as to why you and Faye were allowed to wander so far away from the compound to find the plants? Did you ever find any? Or do you think that they allowed you to easily escape?"

"I never thought they would let us leave." She shrugged

and shook her head. "I don't know."

"Did you get to know any of the children?"

"Two girls from Cancun—Marisa and Delores. I didn't meet them until we were on the boat."

"Do you know their last names?"

"Not anymore. I think they told me once, but I've forgotten. I'm sorry."

"It's okay, Lucinda. You are doing great. I think Elegio has been taking so many notes that his hand is cramped. Right, Elegio?"

The other agent held up the hand holding a pen and tried to flex his fingers but they remained curled like claws. "I'm maimed for life."

The man's humor was not lost on Lucinda. She giggled.

"About ..." Carlos snapped his fingers, trying to remember the names of the girls.

Elegio quickly interjected, "Marisa and Delores."

Carlos nodded, then looked at Lucinda. "Do you know if they were kidnapped?"

"No. They were sisters. Their family was poor and had too many children to feed. Some men told the mother and father the girls could go away to learn a trade and earn money to send home to help the family. The men promised to take good care of the girls. In five years, the sisters would be free to return. So Marisa and Delores were told by their parents they had to go with the men."

"Are these girls still at the compound?"

"Yes."

"Do the children have beds? Do they eat together?"

"Yes, there are beds. But not enough. We share them. Everyone has chores. If you do your chores, there is no problem. You get to eat and have free time to play outside."

"Does anyone try to run away?"

"Where would you run? The jungles here are filled with wild animals that could eat us. And men with guns who would rape and maybe kill us."

"Did you see men?"

"Sometimes, I saw men with big guns. Four or five of them in a truck. They slowed, watching the children playing ball, but they didn't stop."

"Which way was the truck traveling?"

"Toward the city."

"The men who brought you here in the boat— Did you ever see them at the compound?"

Lucinda shook her head. "A truck was waiting at the dock when we arrived. We were put into the truck by the driver who paid the other men. Then we drove away."

"Is there anything else you can tell us about your captors that can help identify them? Anything at all. No matter how unimportant you may think it is."

She shook her head again. "But if I remember something, I'll tell Deanne and Alicia."

"It is a deal, Lucinda. You have a very good memory, and I am sure the information will help us rescue the rest of the children. Thank you."

"You're welcome." Her feet started making little circles again. "What will happen to them?"

"We'll return them to their families."

"Maybe they are just like me and don't have families."

Carlos stepped closer and leaned over, resting his hand on his shoulder. "We will do everything possible to help all of them find homes. Including you."

"You don't need to worry about me. I'm going home with Faye."

Carlos glanced up at me.

He probably expected me to confirm her statement. But I could only shrug. I had no idea if the Franklins would take her with them. I hoped so. "Hey, guys, I want to return to our room," I said. "Dr. Franklin arrived when we were coming to your room. I am anxious to talk to him. I need to find out how soon we can leave."

"Will you get that information to us so we can plan a time to rescue the children?" Carlos asked.

"Do you have a plan?"

"Not yet. We need to sit together and talk about everything we know. I also want to have someone check out the docks for a man called Mateo that has a scar on his face and his left arm and hand."

"Do you know where you will take the children who are from different countries?"

José turned to me. "Ricardo is working on that now."

"Alicia, I am going to our room. I will send Sandy here so she can listen to the discussion."

"Tell her to bring some snacks."

I was surprised to see Faye walking slowly with her Dad on one side and her mother on the other. Faye was blessed to have such wonderful parents. My mother always kept me safe.

My father was an alcoholic. After the age of ten, I never felt he could or would keep me safe. I was forty-three when acute alcoholism "shrunk his brain," as his doctor said. With a memory like a sieve, my father proposed to me, completely unaware I was his daughter.

Now, watching the loving support of Faye's parents, I had tears in my eyes. I scrubbed them away just as Ida reached out her right arm and hugged me, pulling me along with their group of three. For the next five minutes, all four of us slowly walked around our room. All could feel the love. This was such an important feeling for healing the body both physically and emotionally. My body relaxed for the first time since leaving Mexico City.

Faye turned to her mother. "I am tired," she said with great effort. Her words still sounded like she had a mouth full of marbles.

"Okay, Honey."

I stepped away from our huddled little group as Ida and Robert guided their daughter to the couch.

Faye's father gave her a hug. "You are doing a good job of healing. A lot of the swelling has subsided. We will go home as soon as you are able."

"When?" Her eyes grew wide.

"Soon, Sweetheart. I am bringing an instrument from the clinic today to check your ears. After that test, I'll know how soon you can travel."

"Will they let you do that?" Ida asked, holding Faye's elbow to steady her as she lowered herself to the cushion. "Wouldn't it raise questions, taking medical equipment out the door?"

"I have already mentioned to them that you have a head cold," he said to his wife, "and we can't risk flying home until your ears are clear."

She grinned. "Clever, Bobby."

He glanced at me, then spoke to Faye. "I must continue my work at the hospital to avoid arousing suspicion. Some doctors came yesterday from another clinic and asked me to teach them more medical techniques. Tomorrow, they are giving me a tour of their facility. But *you* are my number one priority so if you need something tell me or your mother."

"Okay." She nodded.

Ida patted her daughter's hand. "So, we could be leaving by Tuesday, maybe sooner!"

"Robert," I said, pulling his attention away from his family. "We need to have some advance notice before our departure. Alicia will need time to disguise the girls for moving them through the streets to the airport."

"The airport! One of the reasons I came back to the hotel was to let your team know our plane won't be waiting for us at Rafael Núñez International. We'll be flying out of Cortissoz Airport in Barranquilla."

I was more than a little taken by surprise. The drive would take us about two-and-a-half hours, adding more danger of being exposed. "Does Ricardo know this?"

"Not yet. My pilot told me an hour ago that something is going on at Núñez. He has been seeing a lot more men in different military uniforms canvassing the airport. Some of the mechanics claim they are cartel posing as armed guards, hassling people, inspecting luggage and planes, sometimes twice, even three times. He suggested moving the empty plane while there were no additional passengers or cargo."

"Smart thinking on his part," I said, but worry nagged at my thoughts. "I am not so sure Faye and Lucinda's escape would trigger such a large-scale manhunt. Something bigger must be happening. Either way, we still could have been caught in it."

I rested my hand on his arm to reassure him. "I was about to call my family to touch base. But I will call Ricardo immediately, if you will excuse me."

I went into the bedroom to find my portable phone. The battery was low. It would need to be charged but I had enough to keep the calls brief. Ricardo thanked me for the information, then asked me if the team meeting had been productive. I told him Lucinda had provided a lot of information, including names that could prove useful. I also filled him in about my call with the factory owner. He was pleased with our progress.

I left messages for Kitty and Michael because they weren't home. I reached Ryan at work. He missed me and was planning a barbecue for when I returned.

"Thanks, Ryan. I appreciate everything you've done while I have been gone. I want to give *you* a party!" After I hung up, I plugged my phone into its charger.

A disturbing thought occurred to me.

The tentative ploy to buy the children might not work if we were up against buyers for the Black Market in body parts.

CHAPTER 26

September 4, 1990
Monday, 11:55 p.m.

After passing the day with whatever we could do to occupy us while we waited for the green light to pack and leave, I could not shake a feeling of uneasiness. We were playing cards, but I couldn't concentrate on the game, making silly mistakes. Alicia noticed I was distracted and asked what was bothering me. I couldn't come up with an answer.

The medical device Robert had borrowed from the clinic allowed him to inspect Faye's inner ear and ear drum. He felt another twelve hours would be sufficient time to clear her to fly. So, we were a "go" for the next day.

The good news brought José, Pete, Carlos and Elegio to our suite for a little celebration. They came bearing a feast of Mexican food, including a couple six-packs of *cerveza* and soda pop to toast our last night together.

Not even a few beers and a full belly had been enough to relax me. I was anxious to be home but that wasn't what had kept me awake, tossing and turning.

I must have dozed off because I suddenly woke up with a dreadful feeling that something was wrong. I waited to see if I would be given any insight, but nothing came. The feeling only got worse.

"Can't sleep?" Alicia murmured.

With Faye occupying the convertible sofa, she and I had to bunk together in the king-size bed, which gave us plenty of room but not when one of us tossed and turned. "Sorry. Go back to sleep."

"Is everything okay?"

"I'm not sure."

She pushed herself up on her elbows and turned on the table lamp. "Deanne, something has been bothering you all day. Now, you're churning up the sheets like milk to butter."

I sank down on the edge of the bed and grabbed my pillow, pulling it to my chest. "That's just it. I sense something but I get no details."

"Whoa. That's pretty existential for me."

I chuckled in spite of myself. "Not my intention, I assure you. Most people think psychic abilities are either on all the time or can be turned on like a light switch. Of course, there is no hard-and-fast rule but, for me, I can get 'hits' that are simply too vague to do anything about them."

"I hate to suggest it, but maybe one of your kids or friends is in trouble."

I shook my head. "No, I have such a strong connection with them I'm sure I would know."

"Call José, if it will set your mind at ease."

"It's almost midnight. I don't want to wake him. If anything happens that we need to know, he'll be at our door in flash."

"Very true," she said.

I sighed heavily. "Bad enough I woke you up. I'll grab a

blanket out of the closet and sleep on the floor for the rest of the night."

"Like hell you will, lady. Don't worry about me. If I have any problems, I think there's a couple beers left in the mini-frig that will solve them."

September 5, 1990
Tuesday, 8:30 a.m.

I was awake but still in bed when I was startled by a persistent knocking on the bedroom door leading to the hallway.

"Deanne! Alicia! It's José!"

"Coming!" I said as loud as I dared, jumping to my feet and running around the end of the bed. I grabbed a shirt and pulled it on over my flimsy nightgown.

As soon as the door opened, José dashed inside. "Pete just called me. Juan and Caesar are dead!"

With a shocked gasp, Alicia sat up and yanked the sheet to her chin.

I felt like I had been punched in the gut. "Why? What happened?"

"I don't know." José could not stop moving, pacing, circling. Crying. "Pete was so upset I couldn't understand him."

"Where are Carlos and Elegio?"

"With Pete. Or he is with them. Or—"

I grabbed his arms gently. "Stop. Take a breath."

He swiped tears away from his eyes. "All I know is Pete and

the others must have left the hotel."

"Together?"

"No. Yes. Maybe." He shook her head. "I don't know! He called. He said they were on their way here. That's all."

"Is everyone coming here to the suite?"

"No. My room."

I didn't think José was in any condition to be alone, but Alicia and I needed to get dressed. And I didn't want to send him in the other room where the girls were still sleeping. "Go and wait for them. Alicia and I will come over in a few minutes."

He nodded. "I—I'll make some coffee for us."

"That's good. See you in a little bit."

As soon as we were alone, Alicia and I hurried to our bags, grabbing fresh clothes.

"I don't want to tell Faye or Lucinda anything." She glanced at the adjoining door that was still closed.

"I agree. They are both fragile and don't need added stress."

The door opened at the same time as someone knocked softly on it. Sandy peeked in and whispered, "What's happened?"

I finished pulling a t-shirt over my head, then waved her in, motioning to close the door behind her.

She tip-toed forward.

"Something has happened. We don't know the details." I buckled the belt on my slacks, then reached for my socks and sneakers. I paused to give her my full attention. "It's Caesar and Juan. Pete said they're dead."

"Oh, my God! No!" Her gaze darted frantically around the room. "I want to get out of here."

"You aren't going anywhere yet. Try not to panic. You are not in any danger."

"How do you know that?"

"I just do. Trust me. Please. Faye and Lucinda are still sleeping, and we don't want them to worry. Go back in the living room and stay with them."

Eyes wide, she looked at me tying my shoe laces. "Where are you going? Don't leave me here!"

"Alicia and I are only going next door to José's room to wait for Pete. Carlos and Elegio are with him. Call us if there is a problem."

"I'm ready," Alicia said, standing at the door to the hall, her hand on the handle.

"Me, too. Let's go."

As a precaution, she checked the hall by cracking the door a couple inches. "It's good."

We hurried out and closed the door. Halfway to the next door, we spotted three men emerging from the stairwell at the far end of the hall. Even though they were in the shadows, I was fairly confident the group was our guys.

José let us in on the first knock.

"Pete's here," I said as I passed him. "I saw them coming down the hall."

"Are you sure it wasn't someone else."

"We'll know in a second, won't we?"

A distinctive staccato knock on the door was their signature. Still, José could not be too careful, checking the peep hole to confirm, then unlocked the door.

Carlos, Elegio and Pete rushed in. They looked like they had seen a ghost. Their eyes were bloodshot and blank.

"You need to sit down." I stepped back to allow them to get by and use the bed for a couch.

They sat in unison.

No one said a word.

I moved the chair by the window to the other side of the bed so I could face the three men. Alicia grabbed the desk chair a few feet away and set it next to me while José leaned against the desk, his hands braced on its top.

Elegio studied his hands, smoothing his thumb over a callus on his palm.

"As you know, we change shifts around five o'clock. Our Jeep sprung an oil leak yesterday afternoon so Pete offered to drive us to the barn. We don't use the headlights for the last six miles to avoid being seen."

"Seen by whom?"

"The guards for the drug cartels. The guards for the compound. *Banditos*. Anyone on the road at night is suspicious. The farmers stick to daylight hours to travel."

Taking the time to explain seemed to relax him a little bit. His words were not as clipped, as if speaking with a tight throat.

"We had an agreement that someone would stand outside the barn and give an 'all clear' signal. But when we arrived, no one was there. We stopped our car and waited. After twenty minutes, Carlos and I got out and slowly made our way to the barn."

"I stayed behind," Pete said. "Couldn't leave the van and risk having it gone when we came back."

"When I was about one hundred feet from the barn door," Elegio continued while he rubbed a hand over his chin. "I ran into a body. I saw he had been shot. I called out to Carlos."

Carlos took over. "Just when I heard him, I found two more men down. No point checking vitals. I knew this was bad news. We hauled ass to the car for weapons. After we told Pete what we saw, the three of us suited up in the Kevlar vests and grabbed extra ammo."

Pete added, "I tried to reach Ricardo with the portable but the jungle blocks the signal."

"Does he know now?" Alicia asked.

Pete nodded. "Carlos got a hold of him while I drove us here."

I could see Alicia wanted to know more about Ricardo's reaction, but she hesitated, then asked them to continue.

"We made our way around the back of the barn, instead of taking a direct route, in case anyone else was around. We saw at least fifteen bodies, some inside."

"Juan and Caesar were caught in the loft. No way out. Both were shot in the head."

The room fell silent. The three men were in shock. We all were. But they had seen the blood, bullet holes and blank stares of lifeless eyes.

There were no words to comfort them.

I heard José sniff, trying not to break down. Carlos, Elegio and Pete were stoic beyond anything I could fathom.

As gently as possible, I attempted to nudge more

information out of them. We needed to find out if the authorities were notified.

José informed us that Ricardo was taking care of it. "He doesn't want us to get involved while the Franklins are still here. Getting them out is first priority. Nothing can jeopardize that."

Alicia sighed. "Any ideas about what happened at the barn? Why would there be *fifteen* bodies?"

"Thirteen," Elegio corrected and swallowed hard before continuing. "Not counting our guys."

"But weren't there only four men at the compound?"

"Lucinda said three men and one woman," Carlos added. "Three. Four. What would it matter? If they suspected they were being watched, they would have notified their boss. He could have sent forty men to take care of the problem. After Juan and Caesar managed to kill thirteen of them, they were outnumbered, taken over and executed before the rest walked away."

Pete said, "I'm not so sure they would have had enough clips to take out that many men. Bodies were all over the place. My guess is they got caught in the wrong place, wrong time. Turf wars."

"Maybe we'll learn more from the video. Elegio grabbed the camera off the tractor. We can review the daily tapes, including the one from yesterday."

The hotel phone rang. Everyone looked at it. José stretched across the desk and answered.

"Yes.... Yes, of course.... We'll be waiting." He hung up and started toward the door. "That was Dr. Franklin. He's next door checking on Faye and wants to talk to us immediately. He wouldn't say why."

José opened the door without waiting for the doctor to knock.

Robert rushed in. "What the hell happened last night?"

Everyone started talking at the same time.

"Quiet!" Somehow, José managed to be louder than the rest, which seemed to surprise him as much everyone else. "Dr. Franklin, I think you already know our team has been watching the children left at the compound in the hope of rescuing them after your family is safely out of the country."

With a wary look, Robert nodded. "Yes, I know a little bit about it. Go on."

"Sir, we lost Caesar and Juan. They were shot last night. Several more bodies were found at the barn where we were conducting the surveillance."

"Christ!" Robert shook his head. "There must be a connection to what I saw at the clinic early this morning. A police car was parked in front, and an officer was speaking to the doctor I have been helping. Both were pretty hot under the collar, but I couldn't understand the conversation because they were talking so fast in Spanish. I don't think either one noticed me going into the clinic."

"Which clinic?"

"*Santa Maria Medico*. Just outside of town. When Dr. Rodriguez came in, he was very upset and told me about a drug war last night where fifteen men were killed. The policeman wanted to be called if anyone comes into the clinic with a gunshot wound. Dr. Rodriguez said if he reported anything to the police, his family would be killed."

"Can the police do anything to him if he doesn't cooperate?"

"Not directly. But the police could ignore trouble at the clinic and not answer any calls for help."

"So, Dr. Rodriguez is caught in the middle," Alicia said. "Welcome to Columbia."

"Good-bye to Columbia!" Robert answered. "Faye should be well enough to leave. I'm calling my pilot to prepare for departure this afternoon."

CHAPTER 27

Robert, Alicia and I returned to the suite and opened the door, almost bumping into Sandy on the other side.

She stepped back. "Dr. Franklin, I was just coming to get you."

Faye was lying on the couch with a washcloth on her forehead. Ida sat at her side. Lucinda hovered nearby.

He rushed past Sandy to get to his daughter. "What happened?"

"She's okay, Bobby. She just had a dizzy spell."

"Hey, Dad-dy," Faye said, her words still garbled.

"Hey there, Honey. How are you feeling?" He picked up her wrist, feeling her pulse.

"Woozy. The room keeps spinning."

"Is it worse or better than before?"

"Um ... I dunno."

"Did she lose consciousness?" he asked his wife.

"Yes, just for a second or two. She stood to go to the bathroom, took a few steps and her knees buckled. Luckily, Sandy was right there and caught her."

"Why was she walking by herself? Why wasn't anyone helping her?"

"D-don't, Dad-dy," Faye begged. "Iissh my fault. I di'n't ashk for he-lp."

He lifted her lids and looked into her pupils. He removed the wet washcloth and felt her forehead. "She's warm. Someone hand me my bag, please."

Lucinda scrambled to obey, grabbing it from the floor several feet away.

He thanked her, opened the bag, withdrew a thermometer and put it in Faye's mouth. He had already returned the medical device borrowed from the clinic so he couldn't check her ears for a reoccurrence of the fluid problems.

But dizziness was one of the signs of an inner ear infection for my kids when they were little. If we discovered she had a fever, I knew we wouldn't be going anywhere.

After a few minutes, Robert removed the thermometer and held it up to read. "Ninety-nine-point-nine."

"That's not too bad," murmured Sandy. "Isn't normal ninety-eight-point-six?

"Faye's temperature is always a little lower than average." Her mother patted Faye's arm. "I'm sure everything will be all right, Sweetheart."

Faye's eyes welled with tears. "I ... wan' to g-go ho-me."

Her father knelt on the floor beside the sofa. "We will. Soon. I promise. Just not today. You've had a little set-back. I might have been pushing you too hard. Let's just give you two more days. Then we'll go to Mexico City."

"Why ... there? I wan' go home."

"Mr. Perez, the man who pulled together the team to find you, has a plan to get you out. Flying to Mexico City from Columbia is not as difficult as leaving here and going to the United States. I have been assisting at the clinic and hospital, so Mr. Perez has made arrangements for me to transport a patient to Mexico City for medical treatment."

"What patient?"

"You! You will be traveling with documents for a woman named Natalia Trujillo who had an accident and cannot speak and needs medical attention you can only receive in Mexico City at the trauma center. Your mother will be with us, too."

"Wha' 'bout Lu-cinda?" She swept a hand in her friend's direction. "Can't leave with-ou' her!"

"We know." He patted her shoulder. "We have made arrangements. She will be with Deanne and Alicia using a false passport."

"Alicia, you and I can be the grandmothers. Sandy and Lucinda can be our granddaughters. Sandy looks more like me and Lucinda looks like you."

"Excuse me, but I am not old enough to be a grandmother. How about we are their mothers?"

"Okay with me." I turned to Sandy and Lucinda. "How does that sound to you two?"

Lucinda nodded eagerly. Sandy gave a thumbs-up.

Tears streamed down Faye's cheeks. "Oh, thank you, thank you, thank all of you!"

I could feel the release of her fear and the anxiety. She now felt hopeful.

"Let's get some medicine in you and some aspirin for the fever," her father said. "Then we'll help you into the bedroom where you can sleep for a few hours."

"No, I-m 'kay here."

He frowned. "Promise me you won't get up without

someone helping you."

Faye crossed her heart twice and gave him a small smile.

"Good, I have to go back to the clinic. I hope you are feeling better by the time I return." He leaned over and kissed her forehead. Then he did the same to his wife. "See you soon."

Watching the three of them made me miss my family. I wanted to echo Faye's plea to go home. I was physically tired from staying focused on our safety and I had not been sleeping well, especially the previous night.

"Well," I said, yawning and stretching my arms over my head. "I don't know about the rest of you, but if no one else is using the bedroom for a nap, then I will."

"Would you mind if I took one, too?" Alicia asked. "I promise not to jostle the bed."

I laughed. "I think it's the other way around. That's a promise I need to make to you."

«—»

Four hours later, Alicia and I rejoined the others in the living room. Faye had stayed on the couch, as instructed, and claimed the room had stopped spinning. She and Lucinda played checkers on a tiny travel set Ida bought in the gift shop.

Robert returned from the clinic with a grim expression.

Ida rose from her chair. "Bobby, what's wrong? Please don't tell me you had more problems at the clinic."

"Yes and no." He set down his medical bag and asked for a glass of water. Lucinda appeared with it.

Realizing Lucinda had just read Robert's thoughts about the

water, I smiled to myself. I also sensed she was trying hard to make herself indispensable to Dr. Franklin and his wife. She did not want them to change their mind about taking her along.

"Thank you very much, Lucinda," he said, accepting the glass and taking several swallows. "I made the arrangements for an ambulance, driver and wheelchair for day after tomorrow."

"Wonderful, dear!" Ida gripped his arm and smiled.

"Yes, that's the good news." He looked apprehensively at his daughter, then at me. "We should continue this conversation in José's room. I'd like the other men to join us."

I nodded. "Of course,"

Ida and Sandy offered to stay with the girls.

A few minutes later, Carlos, Elegio and Pete joined us in the other hotel room after José had called them.

Robert told them about the arrangements for the ambulance, then continued with the rest of his news that had not wanted Faye or Lucinda to hear. "A doctor asked me to look at his patient who had been shot."

"Did he know you already knew about the shootout?" I asked.

"No. I wanted to gather any information I could get. I also requested someone handle the translation. The doctor spoke some English and I could tell he was somewhat offended. I explained to the doctor I wanted to fully understand the medical problem. This is always done when you are not fluent in a language. The doctor agreed and found a nurse who could translate for me."

"Was she fluent in English and Spanish?"

Robert nodded. "She had gone to school both in the states and Mexico. She married a Columbian doctor and has lived in Columbia for five years. She's a 'no bullshit' kind of lady. She told the injured man if he wanted to be healed, he'd better tell the truth. I understood bits and pieces of the conversation. She told the man I was a famous doctor from the states."

"Did you know her?" Alicia asked.

"No. I consulted with her husband on another patient who is pregnant with her first child. This patient was having irregular heartbeats. I had some heart medication that I brought with us that corrected the problem."

"Do you usually bring heart medicine?" Alicia asked.

"Yes. Because at the clinics, we see many patients who have heart problems."

I was eager for him to continue with the important details. "What did the man who was shot say?"

"First, he spoke in a very low voice. He said if they knew he talked that he, his new wife and child would be killed. I was glad the nurse could translate as the man spoke so softly I could not hear him. The nurse whispered his responses in my ear as I worked."

"What did his doctor say?"

"Nothing. I doubt he could hear the man any better than I could. I was standing next to him and I could barely hear. And there is nothing wrong with my hearing." Robert pointed toward an ear and flashed a quick grin. "I asked the man if he knew who shot him and where did this happen? The man told me he was shot by a rival drug cartel. He gave the location of an abandoned barn next to the orphanage."

"Orphanage. Ha!" José snorted in disgust.

"Were you able to get the man's name?" Carlos asked.

"Adolph. He didn't know his date of birth or where he was born, but he thought he was about nineteen. He never attended school and was illiterate. He said the night of the shooting he drove the truck and was ordered to stay in it until his group came back. He heard shooting. He got out of the truck and that was when he was shot."

Carlos folded his arms across his chest. "Did he see who shot him?"

"No. He was unconscious until he woke up in the hospital. He said the men had machine guns and he heard rapid firing."

"Do you know where he lives?"

"He said he lives between the fields of coca plants and the orphanage."

"Did he give you a location?"

"He told me you had to drive on an old crumbled and isolated road. He said the fields are invisible to the public. He said if you travel near the fields, you better be with someone who is known. The guards will shoot a trespasser and ask questions later."

"Did you ask him about the children?" I asked.

"Yes. But I was very careful not to arouse any suspicion. He told me there were both boys and girls and they ranged in age from eight to twenty. I asked him if the children were treated okay, and he told me he lived there five years ago and he was treated okay as long as he did what he was told."

"Did he say where the children came from?"

"He didn't know but when he was there, he said most kids were very poor. They were happy to have something to eat every day. He told me his parents gave him to the group because they could not feed him."

Alicia frowned. "How sad for everyone."

"I asked the man if his baby was a boy or girl. With great pride he said the child was a boy. I asked him if he would make sure his son had a less dangerous occupation."

"What did he say?"

"He didn't understand what I was asking. He said he never went school, and he was doing okay."

"I am so grateful for having all the opportunities I've had."

Everyone nodded in agreement.

"The young man was grateful he had a steady job and could care for his family."

"Did he know any of the children or the people caring for the children?"

"The adults are the same ones who cared for him. He didn't know any of the children or where they were from."

"Who did he think the men were who were in the barn?"

"This is where it gets interesting. He said they were from a rival gang that was trying to take over their fields, drug route and protection."

"Who told him it was a rival gang?"

"He said the big man, the chief of everything."

"Did he give you a name?"

"No. He called him *Jefe*. I know that means 'Chief'. But that's the only name he knew."

Pete shifted from one foot to the other, clearing his throat.

"What about Juan and Caesar?"

"All the bodies are in the hospital morgue, including theirs," Robert said solemnly.

José added, "Ricardo is sending a courier with their photographs that I will give to you."

Carlos spoke to Robert. "You will need to be extra careful locating them to get the identifying numbers for Ricardo. No one can suspect you have any ties to them. Ricardo can contact Dr. Rodriguez after your flight takes off and arrange to have their bodies transported."

"Thanks for helping us."

"I wish I could do more."

CHAPTER 28

September 6, 1990
Wednesday, 6:00 a.m.

Alicia, Sandy and I woke early and began going through the trunk of disguises. We were happy to have something to do. Lucinda would be going home with the Franklins. She was excited and looking forward to a new beginning. Her maturity amazed me. I remember being pretty self-centered when I was thirteen years old.

"Hey, are you having a party without us?" Faye and Lucinda staggered into the bedroom, rubbing their eyes and yawning.

"We're getting ready for tomorrow," Sandy said, "What do you think of this wig?"

"I'll wear whatever wig you want me to wear." Lucinda looked at the disguises with fascination.

"Do you ... think we'll be safe?" Faye was still yawning and talking at the same time.

Sandy gave a squeal of delight and ran over to the girls. "Faye! You're talking!"

She grinned as Sandy hugged her. "The swelling went down a lot last night. Must have been the medicine Dad gave to me."

Her speech was not perfect but it was good enough for us

to understand her.

"That's wonderful news!" I hugged her.

Then Alicia gave one, too.

"In answer to your question, from what I can sense, yes, we'll be safe."

"That's good to know. I had scary dreams last night. I remember the man at the compound talking about the violence. He said they were fighting for control of the port."

Alicia moved to stand in front of Faye. "Who was the man talking to?"

"An older white man who came to the compound."

"Did they know you were listening?" she asked.

"No. I was lying down behind some boxes. I didn't feel good and I was trying to rest. I only heard part of the conversation before they went inside the office."

"Had you seen the man before that day?"

Faye shook her head. "I would have remembered. And he had a gruff voice."

"Gruff?" Alicia pursed her lips.

She nodded. "Gravelly. Raspy. You know ... Gruff." She sighed heavily. "I will be so happy when all this over. I just want to get home. I'll never leave the United States again. I acted stupidly in Cancun by not staying with my girlfriends."

"I hope you don't mind my asking," Sandy said, "But why *did* you go with the guy at the club?"

"I don't remember going anywhere with him. I only remember dancing and talking to him, and then waking up in a locked room."

"Did you know where you were?"

"I was told I wasn't in Mexico. I didn't know if it was day or night. There weren't any windows."

"Were there other girls with you?" Alicia asked.

"I didn't see any, but I did hear a girl screaming in pain. I was told the same thing would happen to me if I didn't behave. I lost track of time. They shoved some food through an opening. At first, I couldn't eat because the stuff looked awful. But then I got too hungry to care what it looked like. One night, they came and got me. Two other girls were with them. They spoke English and Spanish."

"Do you speak Spanish?"

"A little. I took classes in high school. I thought I knew more than I actually did." She gave a disparaging snort. "I thought I knew a lot of things. Boy, was I wrong. Now I want learn how I can help prevent children from being kidnapped and having to experience what I did."

"Maybe you should consider law enforcement," Alicia suggested. "Or take investigation classes and call me when you've completed college. I worked as a federal investigator for the United States government before I started my own agency. I work some human trafficking cases. Unlike you, many of the people are from poor counties. No formal education. Their documents are taken away so they cannot leave. Their captors make threats to them about their families."

"But why do they go with them in the first place? I mean, I had no choice."

"They are told they will work in hotels or restaurants. In most cases, they earn nothing. Some of the people are used as domestic labor or factory workers. They work even if they were sick and are kept in isolation."

Lucinda spoke up. "I was told I would learn to be a ma-soose."

Faye grinned. "Masseuse," she corrected.

"Yeah. That's what I said. Mah-soose. They said I would learn how to massage. I already knew a little bit from my mama. But then a woman named Juanita taught me more. But for men, massage meant sex. I did not know until my first appointment with a man. He said he paid for sex, not just some little girl rubbing lotion on him." She shuddered, wrapping her arms around herself. "The men forced me to do things ... It hurt so much. In front and in back. They made me bleed. And my body hurt after that whenever I peed or pooped. I told Juanita I didn't like massage, and I wanted to work in a hotel like my mother."

Faye added, "That's when I met Lucinda. We were both in pain. I talked about wanting to go home. She told me she didn't have a home since her mama died."

As I was listening, my stomach began to twist into knots. Both of these young girls would need counseling. I was sure the Franklins would see to it. Meanwhile, they were both being very brave to even speak of the horrors they'd endured.

"Alicia, I don't know how you can work this type of case," I said.

"I feel I can help these children. I didn't say it was easy."

"If you two hadn't worked this case," Faye said with a sniffle, "I *would* be dead. I already felt dead inside. Lucinda kept me going. She brought me food and water and encouragement. Nobody else wanted to be near me."

Sandy murmured under her breath, "It must've been a living hell."

"It was," Faye said quietly.

"But some kids weren't treated as bad as Faye," Lucinda said. "Some were looking forward to a better life. They weren't hungry. They were learning to write their names, how to use sewing machines, to cook and clean. They were eager to earn some money."

"Did any of them have any idea what was in store for them?" Alicia asked. "Was there ever any talk, any rumors about anything bad about where they would be sent?"

Lucinda shrugged. "When children left, they didn't come back to tell us what happened. Juanita told me everything depended upon how good we were at the jobs we learned."

"Juanita sounds like she was nice to you," I said.

"She was nice to all of us. She gave us a treat if we did a good job."

"What happened if you did a bad job?"

"Those kids were put in a room and sat alone until she came and got them. I never went, though. She said I was smart and that I always did a good job. She didn't punish me, even when I told her I didn't want to do massage anymore."

"Did you tell her about the bleeding?"

Lucinda nodded vigorously. "She got mad. Not at me, though. She told me I didn't have to do massage anymore. And then she gave me some cream to put on down there, front and back. It helped a lot."

"Did she tell you what you would be doing instead of massage?"

"Cooking! At a nice restaurant or hotel. I like fixing food. She said my pay depended on where I went and how good of a cook I was."

Smiling, Faye leaned forward. "Lucinda is a good cook. She brought me food she had prepared just for me. She's the sister I never had."

Lucinda beamed, then turned to Alicia. "If I am good enough at cleaning and cooking and helping Faye, I am hoping her parents will not change their minds about adopting me."

Alicia lit up. "Is it official?"

Faye and Lucinda nodded in unison, then giggled.

My heart leapt to my throat. I reached out and turned Lucinda to face me.

She looked up, complete innocence filled her face.

"I am so happy for you. And your new family. But you don't have to work for their approval. They will love you just as you are. And if something happens and they don't adopt you, I know someone will."

Her big, dark eyes gazed into mine. I heard her silent plea. *You?*

If it is meant to be, yes.

«——»

An hour later, Ida joined us for breakfast in the suite, bringing fresh pastries and orange juice from a bakery. She took a sip of coffee and grimaced. "If there is one thing I miss most, it is a good cup of fresh-ground coffee instead of these hotel packets."

"Ironic, isn't it?" Alicia asked with a wide smile. "We are in

Columbia, home of the world's best coffee beans. And those packets say, 'Made in U.S.A.'."

"That's one of the reasons why I have been itching to get out of this hotel." Sandy dramatically grasped her throat. "I want Columbian coffee!"

"I'll buy you a pound of beans when we get back to the States," I teased. "Columbian. I promise."

"I'll hold you to it!"

"When will we go back to looking at the disguises, Alicia?" Faye was practically bouncing in her seat on the sofa.

What a difference in her energy in one day. And her speech!

"If everyone is finished eating, we can start now." Alicia headed toward the adjoining door to the bedroom as the rest of us followed. She went over to the trunk and lifted the lid. "Take your pick."

"You have quite a collection," Ida said. "How do you plan on hiding Faye's blonde hair?"

Alicia pulled out a skullcap. "We'll put the hair inside the cap. We were hoping you would wrap the skullcap with gauze for the appearance of a head injury." She looked at Faye. "You will need to lean your head down and forward like you have little energy, so nobody can see your face clearly."

"What is Lucinda going to wear?" Ida asked.

"Lucinda will come with us while you and your husband take Faye in the wheelchair to the ambulance. We will go to our car and wait until we see the ambulance pull away from the hotel. Then we will follow you to the Barranquilla."

"Are you changing Lucinda's appearance?"

"Absolutely."

Ida smiled. "It sounds like you ladies have this all worked out."

"Alicia is the best at changing a person's appearance," I said. "Tomorrow morning, you will not recognize your own daughter."

"Make that 'daughters'," Ida corrected. "I have two now." She put an arm around Faye and an arm around Lucinda, giving them each a squeeze.

Both girls giggled. For all that they had been through, they were both getting a wonderful new start.

Alicia started laying clothing on the table. She was a real pro switching items around, mixing and matching for different looks. After fifteen minutes, she was ready. "Faye, this is what you will wear. We will need about an hour to dress you. So, what do you think?"

"It's great!" she clapped her hands. "I'm so ready to be outta here, I would wear a cardboard box if you asked me."

"Brilliant idea!" Sandy laughed as she made the motions of packing a box. "Forget disguises. Stick them in a box and slap on some postage. Why didn't I think of that?"

After we figured out what everyone planned to wear, we spent the rest of the morning just like so many others. Games. Reading. Cards. Girl-talk. We were discussing what we should do for lunch when a knock sounded on the door.

"I bet that will be José, asking if he can get something for us to eat," Sandy said, jumping up to answer it. Without bothering to look through the peep-hole, she unlocked the door and swung it open. "Perfect timing, Jos—. Oh, Dr. Franklin!"

He entered the room in a rush.

Ida stood. "Bobby! What a nice surprise! You're just in time for lunch with all of us girls."

I saw the strain on his face. Something was wrong.

Ida saw it, too, and her smile faded. "Did something happen?"

"I was the hospital when a young boy was brought in. A bag of drugs broke open inside his body." Dr. Franklin began to cry softly. "There was nothing I could do to save him."

"Did he have family with him?" Alicia asked.

He shook his head. "A man was seen carrying him unconscious into the lobby. He left him and took off before anyone could stop him. Dr. Rodriguez found me because the boy was in cardiac arrest. We rushed him into surgery but it was too late. I lost him!" Robert pinched the bridge of his nose as he sighed heavily. "Dr. Rodriguez started cutting down the abdomen from the chest incision. I didn't know what the hell he was doing, mutilating the body like that. I tried to stop him but he peeled back the skin and—" Robert shook his head. "The kid had plastic bags of drugs inside the abdominal cavity! One of the bags had burst."

Ida slipped her arms around his waist and hugged him. "Oh, Robert, I'm so sorry."

He closed his eyes tight but tears still leaked out. He rested his cheek on his wife's head.

Ida murmured, "What did Dr. Rodriguez say?"

"He told me he had seen another young boy who was stuffed with drugs and had died. I have been to many poor countries but this is a first."

Ida and Faye put their arms around Dr. Franklin.

I watched Lucinda get up from her chair and embrace Faye. I was so happy Lucinda was going home with the Franklins. She would have opportunities she would never have had if she remained in Mexico.

Alicia and I went into the bedroom.

Sandy sat on the bed, shaking a bottle of nail polish in one hand. "Ida bought it for me. Thought I'd give them their space and give myself a pedicure. Want to borrow it when I'm done?"

Alicia shook her head. "No thanks. Knock yourself out."

I moved a pillow at the head of the bed and sat, leaning my head back against the headboard. "I'll just rest my eyes for a few."

Several minutes later, Robert came to the open doorway, giving the door a light tap with his knuckles.

At the sound, I opened my eyes.

"May I speak to you for a minute?" he asked.

"Sure," Alicia said.

Sandy glanced between the three of us. "Is that my cue to leave? Again?"

Robert shook his head and motioned for her to stay put. He shoved his hands in the front pockets of his slacks, walking into the middle of the room, facing all of us. "I have some other information I didn't want to share in front of the girls. Dr. Rodriguez told me the other boy who died was found near the compound."

"Does Dr. Rodriguez know what is going on there?" I asked.

"Yes, I think so. I didn't tell him my daughter and Lucinda had been there, too." He raked his hand through his hair. "I don't know who I can trust."

"I know this should go without saying," Alicia said, taking a moment to connect with all our gazes, "But, at this point, we all need to be very careful."

"I can hardly wait to leave." He shook his head slowly. "I don't want Faye or Lucinda to be traumatized anymore. Ida is not sleeping at night, and I am concerned about her wellbeing, too."

"We are all anxious to leave. What time will the ambulance be here tomorrow morning?"

"I ordered it for five a.m."

"Good," I said. "Pete will have a seven-passenger van in the front parking lot. At 4:30. Alicia, Sandy, Lucinda, José and I will go downstairs with him and wait in the van to follow you to the airport."

"What happened to our old brown van?" Alicia wondered.

"For one, it doesn't have enough seats for all of us," I said. "More important, the striped paint makes it a little too out-of-the-ordinary."

"Besides, it's being donated to the clinic." Robert grinned. "I am meeting my pilot and medical technician there in an hour to pick up my equipment. They'll take everything to the plane, including all of your equipment from the van."

"*Our* equipment?" Alicia glanced at our few belongings in the bedroom.

"José said he had some things in a van he'd like us to transport to Mexico City."

"Good old José," Sandy said as she blew on her nails. "Always on the ball, that guy."

"Sounds like all the loose ends are being wrapped up. I don't want to think of anything tomorrow except getting all of us safely on the plane and out of here."

"I am so homesick," Sandy said. "I want a big cheeseburger with French fries and a large Coke. I want to take a long bath, sleep in my own bed and talk for hours with my friends. I dream about it every night."

We walked out of the bedroom with Robert. He gave Ida and Faye a hug and a kiss, then started for the door. "Okay, ladies, I will see you later. When I return, I will bring the wheelchair and gauze."

After the door clicked shut, Alicia began looking at Lucinda's hair. "Do you want to wear a skull cap with a wig, or cut your hair short and change the color?"

"Faye, what do you think?" Lucinda asked, her hands tugging on the end of a long strand.

"Wear a skullcap like me. Then you wear the wig and I'll wear the gauze," Faye said in a sing-song voice, moving her arms back and forth as if she were performing a pirate jig.

Lucinda laughed and clapped, then stopped suddenly. "What will I do?"

"About what?" Faye asked.

"I am afraid if I make a mistake, I'll look like I don't belong with Deanne and Alicia. What if someone notices?"

Faye looked at me and smiled. "Listen to what they tell you to do. They won't let anything bad happen."

"Just remember," I said, "no talking after we leave this

room until we are safe in the car."

She continued to fidget with her hair. "What if I see somebody looking at me funny, like they know me from somewhere?"

Sandy winked at me. "Sounds like *déjà vu*, Deanne?"

I nodded. "Trust me, Lucinda. We've done this scenario before and everything worked out fine. We'll walk together as mother and daughter, holding hands. If you hear or see something, say 'Mom' and squeeze my hand. And with your head, you can give a little nod in the direction you want me to look. Not too much. Just enough for me to know where to look."

"Try this, Lucinda," Sandy offered as she stood and demonstrated. "Pretend we are all on a shopping trip, and we like looking at all the stuff in the shops and windows. That way you won't be tempted to stare at every stranger, wondering if they recognize you."

"Good idea," Alicia said.

Ida shook her head and gave a dramatic wave of her hand. "What a life you have, Alicia. You, Deanne and Sandy. You risk all kinds of danger like some kind of modern-day female versions of Indiana Jones. And yet, after I've spent all this time with you, you're all as normal as any woman I know back home. If I were to bump into you on the street, I'd think you were PTA moms or housewives or ... me!" She pointed to her chest. "I would never guess you were the kind of adventurous dare-devils that you are."

Sandy cracked up, slapping her thigh. "I'm sorry. I mean no disrespect, Mrs. Franklin. But I just never saw us that way. I mean, we spent so much time *pretending* to be *shopping!* That was our cover, anyway. And suddenly, I got this image of Deanne in a brown fedora swinging from a rope in the jungle with a monstrous boulder bearing down on her. That's hysterical!"

Alicia grinned. "Deanne, you have to admit that is funny."

I smiled. "I may have to buy a fedora."

Sandy offered, "You buy me the Columbian coffee. I'll buy you a fedora."

"Well, you do make a great team," Faye said.

"And we wouldn't have been a great team without the backing of your parents," I added.

Faye leaned her head on her mother's shoulder. "I feel blessed to have such a supportive family. Why do you think I was so lucky and many of the children I met didn't have even basic needs met, such as food, water and a safe environment?"

"Faye, an experience such as you had will have a profound effect on your psyche," I said. "Don't let this make you a victim."

"Her dad and I will make sure the experience helps her grow into maturity. We have kept her sheltered and innocent. We feel responsible for not warning her of potential dangers. We are thinking of what we can do to teach young people how to travel in foreign countries."

Alicia spoke. "This is the type of investigation I do fifty percent of the time. I can give you lots of information."

"Alicia is one of the best."

"That would be terrific."

"We need the help."

A knock at the door launched Sandy to her feet. When she

swung open the door, she announced, "About time you got here! I'm starving!"

José and Pete stood in the doorway, each with a tray of food. They glanced at each other with wrinkled brows, then at her.

"How did you know it was us?" asked José.

Pete added, "And how did you know we brought lunch?"

"Woman's intuition, guys. Woman's intuition."

CHAPTER 29

September 7, 1990
Thursday, 1:00 a.m.

"Are you awake?" I asked Alicia in a quiet voice.

"I was restless. I kept waking up and going over things in my mind. I had a hard time turning it off."

"Me, too." I flipped on the lamp by the bed. Clearly, we weren't going back to sleep.

"I am anxious to leave. I received a phone call yesterday about an assignment in the Philippines. A seven-point-eight earthquake occurred in central Luzon. Do you want to join me?"

"Doing what?"

"Whenever lives are lost in a big disaster, the children are at risk of being kidnapped."

"Where are the parents?" I shook my head. "I must be more tired than I thought. Of course, they might be injured."

Alicia grimaced. "Or killed."

I was trying to figure out how she fit in. "What do you do?"

"I help get the children to a safe environment."

"I wish I could take you up on the offer, but I need to go home for several reasons. One, I have a new relationship in my life, and two, my daughter is still in high school. If I can help from home, I'll do what I can. Just let me know."

"Thanks."

Faye was yawning as she and Lucinda stumbled around the corner of the bedroom doorway. She looked great on the outside. I wondered if her entire body was healing so nicely. "I'm ready, what can I do?"

"Get dressed and eat something," Alicia said, "We will do the skullcap last because wearing it can get uncomfortable with all of your hair tucked inside."

Sandy wandered in. "Alicia, I couldn't help but overhear the news about the earthquake in the Philippines. Is there a place for an investigator's apprentice?"

"Are you sure?" Alicia's eyebrows rose. "The hours are long. Sometimes you work fourteen to sixteen hours in one day."

"Now I know what's involved, I'll be more prepared to entertain myself." She grinned, then became serious again. "I can't stop thinking about what can happen to the children. I want to help prevent this atrocity."

Alicia looked at me. "Is that okay with you, Deanne?"

"I don't have any cases needing her assistance now. Since she needs more hours of investigation, she could use the experience."

Sandy clapped her hands. "Cool! I actually have another assignment!"

"But I thought you were anxious to get home," I said.

"Oh, I am! I'd love to crash in my own bed and sleep for two or three days. But I didn't know what I was going to do after that, except go back to work at the temp agency."

Alicia gave a half-hearted smile. "You could end up sleeping on the ground in Luzon."

"That's okay." She shrugged. "This past month, I haven't slept for more than six hours every night. I'll sleep on the plane."

"It must be nice to be young," I groaned playfully. "I'll need four or five days before I feel normal again."

"Why? This certainly wasn't hard labor."

"When I am working a case, especially if there is possible danger, I sleep lightly."

《——》

Nearly an hour passed when I heard a slight tap at the exterior door. I looked through the security peep hole to see José and Pete with another tray of cut-up fruit, little boxes of breakfast cereal and a large stainless-steel pitcher of milk.

I let them in. "You should open a catering company."

Sandy thought this was hysterically funny. So did Faye and Lucinda.

"Let's eat," Pete said, "and we'll take your bags to the car. I already checked us out."

An hour and a half later, at three-thirty, Robert and Ida joined us in our room, bringing a small, rickety wheelchair with them.

"Did you go to bed last night?" Robert asked, looking at his daughter and Lucinda.

"Yes, but we woke around one. We couldn't sleep."

Sandy jiggled the wheelchair. "It's a good thing Faye doesn't weigh very much."

"This was the best I could find at the clinic," Robert said. "It will work well enough to carry her to the curb."

Lucinda and Sandy came out of the room dressed. Alicia immediately went to work changing their appearances. When the transformation was complete, they looked like typical American girls with pony tails and freckles.

"Good job, Alicia," I said. "What are you doing on Halloween?"

Alicia laughed. "I love that holiday. I do make-up for my friends."

Faye came out of the bathroom wearing a hospital gown. "I am ready for the change."

Alicia helped her to a stool, then began putting her hair under the skullcap.

Dr. Franklin stepped forward, carrying a roll of gauze and tape. "Are you ready for me yet?"

"She's all yours." Alicia backed up from Faye and sat, looking at everyone. "She needs some bruises."

"I don't think that is necessary," Robert said. "I brought a blanket from the hospital to cover her. The distance from this room to the entrance to the hotel is limited. We have fresh clothes for her in the plane."

"The soldiers will still be downstairs and at the airport." I scrutinized Faye's new look and nodded my approval. "But they will not be paying much attention to a doctor and his patient."

José added, "After we board, I will call Ricardo on my cellular phone just before we take off to let him know we are safe. I understand a team is already in place ready to rescue the children in the compound."

"Do you know how they plan to rescue the children?"

"No. The only thing I know is they will proceed after we leave."

At four-thirty, Alicia, Sandy, Lucinda and I followed José and Pete to the parked vehicle. We didn't see anyone in the lobby, not even the clerk. Soldiers stood outside but they talked among themselves and didn't pay us any attention. Thirty minutes later, we saw Robert, Ida, the ambulance driver and Faye emerge from the lobby, moving toward the ambulance parked at the curb.

They were putting Faye inside the ambulance when I saw one of the soldiers approach the attendant. I observed the body language. I couldn't sense danger or alarm. After a few minutes, he returned to where the other soldiers were standing.

"Wow. That was scary," Sandy said with great relief.

When the ambulance pulled out, Pete waited to follow at a discreet distance. He didn't want the guards to see us tailing the ambulance. Once we were away from the hotel, he sped up to follow more closely. At this early hour, the roads were empty of traffic. I saw soldiers standing by the side of the road, casually talking. The sight of men with guns everywhere made me glad to return to the U.S.

After we arrived at the airport in record time, Robert handled all of the talks with the officials. He was respected and known for his good work helping the local people.

We managed to pass by the officials without arousing suspicion and boarded the plane.

Sandy sank into a seat and sighed heavily. "I will be so glad when we take off and leave this place behind. I can't help but worry something bad could still happen."

I sat down next to her and patted her arm. "I keep focusing on us arriving safely in Mexico City. I have been afraid but I won't allow the fear to run my emotions."

"And how do you do that?"

"First, I admit to myself I am afraid. Next, I ask myself if the threat is real. When I have the correct answer, I act accordingly."

Sandy raised her brows. "How do you know if the fear is real?"

"I ask myself if this feels real."

Across the aisle, Ida unwrapped the gauze from her daughter's head and face.

Faye smiled from ear to ear. "I can't believe I am actually going home. This is the happiest day of my life."

I leaned closer to Sandy. "Do you feel her joy?"

"Who wouldn't?"

"Is that joy real or imagined?"

"Real."

I pointed at Sandy and winked. "That is the difference."

《—》

Our plane arrived in Mexico City at two-thirty in the afternoon. José and Pete looked as relieved as the rest of us to be on the ground. Ricardo was waiting at the airport to take us to an executive lounge to talk privately. He had a wheelchair waiting for Faye to avoiding tiring her out any more than she already was.

The Franklins would stay overnight to allow Faye a chance to rest before they continued home. The day had been long, and the exhaustion was beginning to show on her face. She could not risk having a relapse.

Ricardo held plane tickets for Alicia, Sandy and me for later in the day, and handed them to us as we walked into the lounge. A bottle of champagne chilled in an ice bucket on the conference table. Fluted glasses were set nearby. Three platters were laid out with cheese, cold cuts, crackers and fruit. He invited us to fill a plate and take a seat around the table.

Two waiters emerged from behind a door, offering a choice of beverages.

Before long, we were all comfortably situated.

"Any word from Carlos and Elegio yet?" Pete said pointedly to Ricardo.

"They joined a large contingency of agents from Mexico that went to the compound. No adults were on the premises. All but eleven children were gone, and those are returning to Mexico. If their own families cannot be located, I will make sure they are placed in good homes."

"What do you think happened to the other children?" asked Sandy looking around at the others.

Alicia answered, "Sounds like someone tipped off the kidnappers, and they moved them to another location."

"But why leave eleven behind?"

"They probably didn't have time to move everyone."

Faye rested her head on her propped-up hand. "I bet they left the younger ones. I overheard Maria telling Papo she didn't know why they took such young children as they were more work than what they were worth."

"How old do you think the youngest child was at the compound?"

"Three or four."

"Ricardo, if we can do anything to help, please call me," Alicia said.

"We will stay in touch, and I will keep you all informed of the outcome."

Ricardo motioned to the waiters, who came forward and opened the champagne bottle, then poured and served the amber liquid to the adults and juice for the girls. We all had a glass in our hand, then Ricardo raised his and offered a toast—first to Faye and Lucinda, for their strength and bravery and will to survive. Glasses were clinked, and sips were taken.

The second toast was to our team—Alicia, Sandy, Pete, José and me—on a job well done, to which the Franklins enthusiastically agreed.

I returned the appreciation toward Ricardo for organizing and directing the successful outcome of finding Faye. Again, everyone raised their glass and cheered.

Though the occasion was a joyous one, it was bittersweet, too. We were not just saying goodbye to new friends, but we all acknowledged the loss of Caesar and Juan. We were sorry we hadn't spent more time with them like with the others. They were a vital part of our team, and they would be forever remembered.

All too soon, the time arrived to say our goodbyes to the Franklins, including Lucinda, who was already one of their family as far as we were concerned. We promised to keep in touch. I invited them to visit me in California, which they promised they would do. After tearful hugs, we went our separate ways. This had been a stressful month, and we were all glad the investigation was over. We had made lasting friendships.

«——»

The flight to LAX from Mexico City was only two hours long. When I stepped out of the jet way, I spotted Ryan, Kitty and Michael all waiting for me. Ryan held a bouquet of red roses.

I walked up to them and gave each of them a big hug. "I am so glad to see you guys. I never want to be gone for this long again!"

Kitty grinned from ear to ear. "Mom, Ryan has a surprise for you."

Ryan stepped closer, flowers in hand. When I accepted them, he wouldn't let go. Instead he leaned over them until his lips were close to mine.

"Welcome home, babe." He kissed me. A brief, sweet kiss. Then he whispered, "To be continued."

Michael cleared his throat.

I grinned. Ryan pretended to act sheepish and pulled back, but only a little. He glanced at my kids, winked, then looked at me again.

"How do you feel about a week in Hawaii?"

"Hawaii? Really?"

"I rented a big house with enough room for all of us—you, me, Michael, Kitty, Bobby and Mark."

What a wonderful way to reconnect with Ryan, my kids and his kids. And I was grateful Ryan had not only come up with the idea but also made all the arrangements.

"That sounds like heaven." I threw my arms around him again, accidentally batting the back of his head with the roses.

He laughed, hugging me tighter. "You said you'd need a couple days to catch up at your office, so we leave the day after tomorrow.

"Thank you!" I kissed him, then turned to Kitty and Michael. "Looks like we're all going to Hawaii!"

《—》

I spent the next day catching up with mail and messages and packing for Hawaii. I tried to contact the Franklins but was unable to reach them. After I left a message on their answering machine, I was contacted by their son, Charles. He reassured me everyone was fine. They were delayed in Mexico City waiting for Lucinda's documentation. I asked Charles to tell them I would call when I returned home in one week.

Hanging up the phone, I felt a nudge at the back of my knee.

"Heidi-girl! I didn't forget you." I knelt and hugged my German Shepherd. She licked my face and made me laugh. "I have a very special person coming over to stay here at the house while we're gone."

Heidi wiggled her whole body and nearly knocked me over. I scratched behind her ears, then checked my watch.

"I figure we have one hour to take a good long walk and maybe even play some ball. Would you like that?"

Her tail wagged as she danced backward toward the front door.

I grabbed her leash and clipped it to her collar. "Kitty! Michael! I'm taking Heidi out before we leave!"

"Okay," they answered in unison from their bedrooms.

Walking out onto my porch, I saw Ryan pull into my driveway. My heart did a little leap. "Are you early or did my watch stop?"

He hopped out and sauntered over, looking me up and down with a twinkle in his eyes. Then he grabbed me around the waist and kissed me. With his lips still close to mine, he murmured, "I couldn't stay away a minute longer."

I smiled and kissed him until I felt another nudge against my leg that swayed both of us.

Ryan chuckled.

"I thought I'd give Heidi some quality time before I leave again.

He stepped aside and slipped his arm around my waist. "A walk would do me good before I sit on the plane for hours. Do you mind if I tag along?"

"Not at all."

As Heidi led the way, we walked and talked about the trip ahead of us. I was so excited to spend an entire week with him and our kids on a beautiful tropical island. There would be plenty of time later to tell him all about finding Faye.

I was looking forward to doing nothing. I'd had enough excitement this past month to last a lifetime.

ACKNOWLEDGMENTS

Deanne Acuña expressed appreciation
to all her friends and family who have supported her
throughout her career.

Sue Phillips would like to express appreciation for
Mindy Neff
Linda Carroll-Bradd of Lustre Editing
Kim Killion of Hot Damn Designs

ABOUT THE AUTHORS

Deanne Acuña was a private investigator licensed by the California Department of Consumer Affairs' Bureau of Security and Investigative Services (BSIS). She is also a Certified Legal Investigator (CLI) through the National Association of Legal Investigators (NALI) and a Certified International Investigator (CII). She is a member of the National Council of Investigation & Security Services (NCISS), the International Intelligence Network (INTELLENET), the California Association of Licensed Investigators (CALI) and the Professional Investigators of California (PICA).

While Deanne was open about her telepathic and claircognizant abilities, she did not promote herself as such, or allow it to cast doubt on her credentials as a certified professional investigator. While telepathy and precognition proved beneficial in her line of work, she relied as much on her common sense as on her sixth sense.

The purpose of the Intuitive Investigator series is to inform and educate readers about how Deanne utilized her acute intuition in her career as well as to focus a spotlight on serious social issues such as drug addiction, human trafficking and elder abuse. With over thirty-five years' experience, she ran a highly successful agency in the Los Angeles area with a select team of associates, including her daughter, Kimberly Acuña.

Deanne passed away suddenly, unexpectedly and peacefully on

November 26, 2018. She is greatly missed by all her friends and family.

«—»

Sue Phillips has been everything from college radio DJ to aerobics instructor at Richard Simmons' Anatomy Asylum. She has counted whales as a member of the Gray Whale census and volunteered at the Cabrillo Aquarium as a Whale Watch Naturalist on board sea excursions off the coast of Southern California.

Published by St. Martin's Press, Jove Books and Harlequin Temptation under various pseudonyms, her novels have been reissued by Sweetbriar Creek Publishing Company. She is a member of Novelists, Inc., Women's Fiction Writers Association, Alliance of Independent Authors and Romance Writers of America.

While her fiction writing has focused on paranormal romantic suspense, she is thrilled and honored to collaborate with Deanne Acuña on two narrative nonfiction novels about Deanne's investigative cases.

For more information about Sue, please visit
https://www.SuePhillipsAuthor.com/
https://www.facebook.com/SuePhillipsAuthorPage
https://twitter.com/SuePhillips_